The Visit

A DRAMA IN THREE ACTS

By Friedrich Duerrenmatt

Adapted by Maurice Valency

SAMUEL FRENCH, INC.
45 WEST 25TH STREET   NEW YORK 10010
7623 SUNSET BOULEVARD HOLLYWOOD 90046
LONDON   TORONTO

THE VISIT was first produced in New York at the Lunt-Fontanne Theatre on May 5th, 1958, under the direction of Peter Brook with the following cast:

CLAIRE ZACHANASSIAN...............*Lynn Fontanne*
BOBBY ....*John Wyse*
PEDRO ....*Myles Eason*
MAX ....*Bill Thourlby*
MIKE ....*Stanley Erikson*
FIRST BLIND MAN................*Vincent Gardenia*
SECOND BLIND MAN................*Alfred Hoffman*
ANTON SCHILL.......................*Alfred Lunt*
FRAU SCHILL.....................*Daphne Newton*
THE SON............................*Ken Walker*
THE DAUGHTER......................*Marla Adams*
THE BURGOMASTER....................*Eric Porter*
THE PASTOR......................*William Hansen*
THE TEACHER....................*Peter Woodthorpe*
THE DOCTOR......................*Howard Fischer*
THE POLICEMAN....................*John Randolph*
THE PAINTER...................*Clarence Nordstrom*
THE FIRST MAN.................*Kenneth Thornett*
THE SECOND MAN.....................*David Clarke*
THE THIRD MAN......................*Milton Selzer*
THE FOURTH MAN...................*Harrison Dowd*
THE FIRST WOMAN................*Gertrude Kinnell*
THE SECOND WOMAN $\Big\}$ ....*Freda Altman*
THE FRAU BURGOMASTER
THE TWO GRANDCHILDREN..*Lesley Hunt, Lois McKim*
THE STATION MASTER................*Joe Leberman*
THE CONDUCTOR................*Jonathan Anderson*
THE REPORTER......................*Edward Moor*
THE PHOTOGRAPHER...................*Lesley Hunt*
THE RADIO REPORTER.............*Vincent Gardenia*
THE CAMERAMAN......................*Ed Moore*
THE TRUCK DRIVER...................*John Kane*
THE ATHLETE...................*James MacAaron*

THE DELIVERY MAN................*Milton Selzer*
FIRST TOWNSMAN ....*Robert Donley*
SECOND TOWNSMAN................*Kent Montroy*

NOTE: Offstage music and sound play an important part in the staging of THE VISIT. A complete music and sound recording, as used in the original New York production, is available on a rental basis. Interested groups should write direct to Masque Sound, 331 West 51st Street, New York, N. Y. 10019, for details.

The Visit

ACT ONE

*A railway-crossing BELL starts ringing. Then is heard
the distant sound of a locomotive WHISTLE. The
CURTAIN rises.*

*The scene represents, in the simplest possible manner, a
little town somewhere in Central Europe. (See Scene
Design # 1.) The time is the present. The town is
shabby and ruined as if the plague had passed there.
Its name, Güllen, is inscribed on the shabby sign-
board which adorns the façade of the railway station
unit, Left. This edifice is summarily indicated by
a small house and a wooden platform facing the
audience, beyond which one imagines the rails to
be. THE THIRD MAN leans on a baggage truck
standing Down Left. In the station wall is a door
with a sign: EINTRITT VERBOTEN. This leads
to the station master's office. Left of the station is
a little house in grey stucco, formerly whitewashed.
It has a tile roof, badly in need of repair. Some
shreds of travel posters still adhere to the windowless
walls. A shingle hanging over the entrance Left
reads: MÄNNER. On the other side the shingle
reads: DAMEN. And under this a torn timetable
marked FAHRPLAN hanging on two nails. Along
the wall of the little house there is a wooden bench,
backless, on which two MEN are lounging cheer-
lessly, shabbily dressed, with cracked shoes. The
PAINTER is busied with paint-pot and brush Down
Left. He is kneeling on the ground, painting a strip of
cloth with the words, WELCOME, CLARA. THE
SECOND MAN is seated on a wooden box near the
station master's office. The warning SIGNAL rings*

5

*uninterruptedly while the sound of the approaching
TRAIN comes closer and closer (SOUND CUE #
1). The* STATION MASTER *issues from his office, advances to the Center of the platform and salutes.
The TRAIN thunders past in a direction parallel to
the footlights, between them and the audience, and
is lost in the distance. The* MEN *on the bench
follow its passing with a slow movement of their
heads, from Left to Right.*

FIRST MAN. The "Emperor." Hamburg-Naples.
SECOND MAN. Then comes the "Diplomat."
THIRD MAN. Then the "Banker."
FOURTH MAN. And at 11:27 the "Flying Dutchman."
Venice-Stockholm.
FIRST MAN. Our only pleasure—watching trains.

(*The station BELL rings. [SOUND CUE # 2.] The*
STATION MASTER *comes out of his office and salutes
the train. The* MEN *follow its course, Right to Left.*)

FOURTH MAN. Once upon a time the "Emperor" and
the "Flying Dutchman" used to stop here in Güllen. So
did the "Diplomat," the "Banker" and the "Silver
Comet."
SECOND MAN. Now it's only the local from Kaffigen
and the 12:40 from Kalberstadt.
THIRD MAN. The fact is, we're ruined.
FIRST MAN. What with the Wagonworks shut down.
SECOND MAN. The Foundry finished.
FOURTH MAN. The Golden Eagle Pencil Factory all
washed up—
FIRST MAN. It's life on the dole.
SECOND MAN. Did you say life?
THIRD MAN. We're rotting.
FIRST MAN. Starving.
SECOND MAN. Crumbling.
FOURTH MAN. The whole damn town—
THIRD MAN. Once we were a centre of industry.

THE PAINTER. A cradle of culture.

FOURTH MAN. One of the best little towns in the country.

FIRST MAN. In the world.

SECOND MAN. Here Goethe slept.

FOURTH MAN. Brahms composed a quartet.

THIRD MAN. Here Berthold Schwarz invented gunpowder.

THE PAINTER. (*Rises, moves to* FIRST MAN.) And I who once got first prize at the Dresden Exhibition of Contemporary Art— What am I doing now? (*Station BELL rings.* [*SOUND CUE # 2A.*] Painting signs!

(STATION MASTER *comes out, throws away cigarette. All rush;* THIRD MAN *gets cigarette and sits Center smoking.* FIRST MAN *moves back to bench, stands, others remain standing around* THIRD MAN.)

FIRST MAN. Well, anyway, Madame Zachanassian will help us.

FOURTH MAN. (*Moves back to bench.*) If she comes.

THIRD MAN. (*Moving toward trolley.*) If she comes.

SECOND MAN. Last week she was in France. She gave them a hospital.

FIRST MAN. (*Sits on bench.*) In Rome she founded a free public nursery.

THIRD MAN. In Leuthenau, a bird sanctuary.

THE PAINTER. (*Crosses Center.*) They say she got Picasso to design her car.

FIRST MAN. Where does she get all that money?

SECOND MAN. An oil company, a shipping line, three banks and five railways—

FOURTH MAN. And the biggest string of geisha houses in Japan. (*Laugh.*)

(*From the direction of the town come the* BURGOMASTER, *the* PASTOR, *the* TEACHER *and* ANTON SCHILL. *They enter Fourth Bay, Left. The* BURGOMASTER, *the*

TEACHER *and* SCHILL *are men in their fifties. The* PASTOR *is ten years younger. All four are dressed shabbily and are sad-looking. The* BURGOMASTER *looks official.* SCHILL *is tall and handsome, but graying and worn; nevertheless a man of considerable charm and presence. He walks directly to the little house and disappears into it.* BURGOMASTER *comes Down Center.*)

PAINTER. (*Crosses to* BURGOMASTER.) Any news, Burgomaster? Is she coming?

ALL. (*They move forward.*) Is she coming?

BURGOMASTER. She's coming. The telegram has been confirmed. Our distinguished guest will arrive on the 12:40 from Kalberstadt. Everyone must be ready.

(MEN *get brooms and start sweeping toward Upper Right.*)

TEACHER. (*To Left of* BURGOMASTER.) The Mixed Choir is ready. So is the Children's Chorus.

BURGOMASTER. And the church bell, Pastor?

PASTOR. The church bell will ring. As soon as the new bell-ropes are fitted. The man is working on them now. (*Speaks to* FIRST MAN.)

BURGOMASTER. The town band will be drawn up in the market place and the Turnverein will form a human pyramid in her honor—the top man will hold the wreath with her initials. Then lunch at the Golden Apostle. I shall say a few words.

TEACHER. Of course.

BURGOMASTER. I had thought of illuminating the town hall and the cathedral, but we can't afford the lamps.

PAINTER. Burgomaster—what do you think of this? (*Shows banner.*)

BURGOMASTER. (*Calls.*) Schill! Schill!

TEACHER. Schill!

SCHILL. (*Enters, stepping over brooms, to Right of* BURGOMASTER.) Yes, right away. Right away.

BURGOMASTER. This is more in your line. What do you think of this?

SCHILL. (*Looks at the sign.*) No, no, no. That certainly won't do, Burgomaster. It's much too intimate. It shouldn't read: "Welcome, Clara." It should read "Welcome, Madame"— (*He hesitates.*)

TEACHER. Zachanassian.

BURGOMASTER. Zachanassian.

SCHILL. Zachanassian.

PAINTER. But she's Clara to us.

FIRST MAN. Clara Wäscher.

SECOND MAN. Born here.

THIRD MAN. Her father was a carpenter. He built the— (ALL *turn and stare at the little house.*)

SCHILL. All the same—

PAINTER. If I—

BURGOMASTER. No-no-no. He's right. You'll have to change it.

PAINTER. Oh well, I'll tell you what I'll do. I'll leave this and I'll put "Welcome, Madame Zachanassian" on the other side. Then if things go well, we can always turn it around.

BURGOMASTER. Good idea. (*To* SCHILL.) Yes?

SCHILL. Anyway it's safer. Everything depends on the first impression. (*Crosses, sits on bench and takes off shoe. The* PAINTER *turns the banner over and goes to work. A TRAIN BELL is heard.*)

FIRST MAN. Hear that? The "Flying Dutchman" has just passed through Leuthenau. (*He and* THIRD MAN *get ladders and start to decorate station.*)

BURGOMASTER. Gentlemen, you know that the millionairess is our only hope.

PASTOR. (*Right of bench.*) Under God.

BURGOMASTER. Under God. Naturally. Schill, we depend entirely on you.

SCHILL. Yes, I know. You keep telling me.

BURGOMASTER. After all, you're the only one who really knew her.

SCHILL. Yes, I knew her.

PASTOR. You were really quite close to one another in those days?

SCHILL. Close? Yes, we were close, there's no denying it. We were in love. I was young—good looking, so they said, and Clara—I can still see her in the great barn coming towards me—like a light out of the darkness. And in the Konradsweil Forest, she'd come running to meet me—barefooted—her beautiful red hair streaming behind her. Like a witch. Oh, I was in love with her all right. But you know how it is when you're twenty—

PASTOR. What happened?

SCHILL. (*Shrugs.*) Life came between us.

BURGOMASTER. (*Gets box and sits Left of bench.*) You must give me some points for my speech. (*He takes out his notebook.*)

SCHILL. Yes, I think I can help you there.

TEACHER. (*Gets box and sits Left of* BURGOMASTER.) Well, I've gone through the school records. And the young lady's marks were, I'm afraid to say, absolutely dreadful. Even in deportment. The only subject in which she was even remotely passable was natural history.

BURGOMASTER. Good in natural history. That's fine. (*He makes a note.*)

SCHILL. She was an outdoor girl. Wild. Once, I remember, they arrested a tramp, and she threw stones at the policeman. She hated injustice passionately.

BURGOMASTER. Strong sense of justice. Excellent.

SCHILL. And generous—

ALL. Generous?

SCHILL. Generous to a fault. Whatever little she had, she shared—so goodhearted. She once stole a bag of potatoes to help a poor widow.

BURGOMASTER. (*Writing in notebook.*) Wonderful generosity—

(FIRST *and* THIRD MEN *move ladders, continue with decorations.*)

TEACHER. Generosity.

BURGOMASTER. That, gentlemen, is something I must not fail to make a point of.

SCHILL. And such a sense of humor! I remember once when the oldest man in town fell and broke his leg, she said, oh dear, now they'll have to shoot him.

BURGOMASTER. Well, I've got enough. The rest, my friend, is up to you. (*He puts the notebook away.*)

SCHILL. (*Rises and crosses to Left station house.*) Yes, I know, but it's not so easy. After all, to part a woman like that from her millions—

BURGOMASTER. Exactly. Millions. We have to think in big terms here.

TEACHER. (*Rises, moves to Left of* SCHILL.) If she's thinking of buying us off with a nursery school—

ALL. Nursery school!

PASTOR. Don't accept.

TEACHER. Hold out.

SCHILL. I'm not so sure that I can swing it. You know, she may have forgotten me completely.

BURGOMASTER. (*He exchanges a look with the* TEACHER *and the* PASTOR, *rises and crosses to* SCHILL.) Schill, for many years you have been our most popular citizen. The most respected and the best loved.

SCHILL. (*Steps forward.*) Why, thank you—

BURGOMASTER. And therefore I must tell you—last week I sounded out the political opposition, and they agreed. In the spring you will be elected to succeed me as Burgomaster. By unanimous vote. (*The* OTHERS *clap their hands in approval.*)

SCHILL. But, my dear Burgomaster—!

BURGOMASTER. It's true.

TEACHER. (*Shakes hands with* SCHILL.) I'm a witness. I was at the meeting.

SCHILL. (*Shakes hands with* FOURTH MAN *and* PAINTER.) This is—naturally, I'm terribly flattered— It's a completely unexpected honor.

BURGOMASTER. You deserve it.

SCHILL. Burgomaster! Well, well—! (*Briskly, at box Center, puts foot on box and arm around* TEACHER'S *shoulder.*) Gentlemen, let's get down to business. The first chance I get, of course, I shall discuss our miserable position with Clara . . .

TEACHER. But tactfully, tactfully—

SCHILL. What do you take me for? We must feel our way. Everything must be correct. Psychologically correct. For example, here at the railway station, a single blunder, one false note, could prove disastrous.

BURGOMASTER. He's absolutely right. The first impression colors all the rest. Madame Zachanassian sets foot on her native soil for the first time in many years. She sees our love and she sees our misery. She remembers her youth, her friends. The tears well up into her eyes. Her childhood companions throng about her. I will naturally not present myself like this, but in my black coat with my top hat. Next to me, my wife. Before me, my two grandchildren, all in white, with roses. My God, if it only comes off as I see it! If only it comes off. (*The station BELL begins ringing.*) Oh, my God! Quick, we must get dressed.

FIRST MAN. (*Comes down ladder, crosses Down Right.*) It's not her train. It's the "Flying Dutchman."

PASTOR. (*Calmly.*) We have still two hours before she arrives.

SCHILL. (*Takes box and sits near Left station house.*) For God's sake, don't let's lose our heads. We still have a full two hours.

BURGOMASTER. Who's losing their heads? (*To FOURTH and SECOND MEN.*) When her train comes, you two, Helmsberger and Vogel, will hold up the banner with "Welcome Madame Zachanassian." The rest will applaud. (FOURTH *and* SECOND MEN *take position on ladders.*)

THIRD MAN. Bravo! (*He applauds.*)

BURGOMASTER. (*Looks at* THIRD MAN.) But, please, one thing—no wild cheering like last year with the government relief committee. It made no impression at all and we still haven't received any loan. What we need here is a feeling of genuine sincerity. That's how we greet with full hearts our beloved sister who has been away from us so long. Be sincerely moved, my friends, that's the secret; be sincere. Remember you're not dealing with a child. Next a few brief words from me. Then the church bell will start pealing—

(*He is interrupted by the thunder of the approaching TRAIN. [SOUND CUE # 3.] The* MEN *crane their heads to see it pass. The* STATION MASTER *advances to the platform and salutes.*)

PASTOR. If he can fix the ropes in time.

(*The station BELL starts to ring.*)

BURGOMASTER. Then the Mixed Choir moves in. And then—
TEACHER. We'll form a line down here.
BURGOMASTER. Then the rest of us will form in two lines leading from the station—

(*There is a screech of brakes. [SOUND CUE # 3A.] The* FOUR MEN *jump up in consternation.* ALL *move Downstage except* SCHILL, *who rises from box.*)

PAINTER. But the "Flying Dutchman" never stops!
FIRST MAN. It's stopping.
SECOND MAN. In Güllen!
THIRD MAN. In the poorest—
FIRST MAN. The dreariest—
SECOND MAN. The lousiest—
FOURTH MAN. The most God-forsaken hole between Venice and Stockholm.
STATION MASTER. It cannot stop!

(*The train noises stop. There is only the panting of the ENGINE. The* STATION MASTER *runs off.*)

PAINTER. It's stopped!

OFFSTAGE VOICES. What's happened? Is there an accident? (*A hubbub of offstage VOICES, as if the passengers on the invisible train were alighting.*)

CLAIRE. (*Offstage.*) Is this Güllen? (ALL *move Upstage, opposite first Bay Left for* CLAIRE'S *entrance.*)

CONDUCTOR. (*Offstage.*) Here, here, what's going on?

CLAIRE. (*Offstage.*) Who the hell are you?

CONDUCTOR. (*Offstage.*) But you pulled the emergency cord, Madame!

CLAIRE. (*Offstage.*) I always pull the emergency cord.

STATION MASTER. (*Offstage.*) I ask you what's going on here?

CLAIRE. (*Offstage.*) And who the hell are you?

STATION MASTER. (*Offstage.*) I'm the Station Master, Madame, and I must ask you—

CLAIRE. (*Enters.*) No!

(*From First Bay Left appears* CLAIRE ZACHANASSIAN. *She is an extraordinary woman. She is in her fifties, red-haired, remarkably dressed, with a face as impassive as that of an ancient idol, beautiful still, and with a singular grace of movement and manner. She is simple and unaffected, yet she has the haughtiness of a world power. The entire effect is striking to the point of the unbelievable. Behind her comes her* FIANCÉ, *tall, young, very handsome, and completely equipped for fishing, with creel and net, and with a rod-case in his hand. An excited* CONDUCTOR *follows.*)

CONDUCTOR. But, Madame, I must insist! You have stopped "The Flying Dutchman." I must have an explanation.

CLAIRE. Nonsense. Pedro—

PEDRO. Yes, my love?

CLAIRE. This is Güllen. Nothing has changed. I recognize it all. There's the forest of Konradsweil. There's a brook in it full of trout where you can fish. And there's the roof of the great barn. Ha! God! What a miserable blot on the map! (*She crosses the stage and goes off First Bay Right with* PEDRO. CONDUCTOR *and* STATION MASTER *cross Down Left to first bay.*)

SCHILL. (*Crosses Down Right.*) My God! Clara!

TEACHER. (*Moves Upstage.*) Claire Zachanassian!

ALL. Claire Zachanassian!

BURGOMASTER. And the town band? The town band! Where is it?

TEACHER. The mixed choir! The mixed choir!

PASTOR. The church bell! The church bell!

BURGOMASTER. (*To the* FIRST MAN.) Quick! My dress coat! My top hat! My grandchildren! Run! Run! (FIRST MAN *runs off Up Right.* BURGOMASTER *shouts after him:*) And don't forget my wife!

(*General panic. The* SECOND MAN *and* FOURTH MAN *hold up the banner on which only part of the name has been painted: WELCOME MA—.* CLAIRE *and* PEDRO *re-enter, Right.* CONDUCTOR *and* STATION MASTER *cross to meet them Down Left Center.*)

CONDUCTOR. (*Mastering himself with an effort.*) Madame. The train is waiting. The entire international railway schedule has been disrupted. I await your explanation.

CLAIRE. You're a very foolish man. I wish to visit this town. Did you expect me to jump off a moving train?

CONDUCTOR. (*Stupefied.*) You stopped the "Flying Dutchman" because you wished to visit the town?

CLAIRE. Naturally.

CONDUCTOR. (*Inarticulate.*) Madame!

STATION MASTER. Madame, if you wished to visit the town, the twelve-forty from Kalberstadt was entirely at your service. Arrival in Güllen, one-seventeen.

CLAIRE. The local that stops at Loken, Beisenbach and Leuthenau? Do you expect me to waste three-quarters of an hour chugging dismally through this wilderness?

CONDUCTOR. Madame, you shall pay for this!

CLAIRE. Bobby, give him a thousand marks.

(*Her* BUTLER, *a man in his seventies, wearing dark glasses, steps forward from Down Left and opens his wallet. The* TOWNSPEOPLE *gasp.*)

CONDUCTOR. (*Taking the money in amazement.*) But Madame!

CLAIRE. And three thousand for the Railway Widows Relief Fund.

CONDUCTOR. (*With the money in his hands.*) But we have no such fund, Madame.

CLAIRE. (*Moving Up Center with* PEDRO.) Now you have.

BURGOMASTER. (*Pushes his way forward. He whispers to the* CONDUCTOR.) The lady is Madame Claire Zachanassian!

CONDUCTOR. Claire Zachanassian? Oh, my God! (*To* CLAIRE.) But that's naturally quite different. Needless to say, we would have stopped the train at once if we'd had the slightest idea. (*He hands the money back to* BOBBY.) Here, please. I couldn't dream of it. Four thousand. My God!

CLAIRE. Keep it. Don't fuss.

CONDUCTOR. Would you like the train to wait, Madame, while you visit the town? The Administration will be delighted. The cathedral porch. The town hall—

CLAIRE. You may take your train away now. I don't need it any more.

STATION MASTER. All aboard! (*He puts his whistle to his lips.*)

PEDRO. (*Stops him.*) But the Press, my angel. They don't know anything about this. They're still in the dining car.

CLAIRE. Let them stay there. I don't want the Press in Güllen at the moment. Later they will come by themselves. (*To* STATION MASTER.) And now what are you waiting for?

STATION MASTER. All aboard! (*The* STATION MASTER *blows a long blast on his whistle. The TRAIN leaves.* [*SOUND CUE # 4.*] *Meanwhile the* FIRST MAN *has brought the* BURGOMASTER'S *dress coat. He puts it on, then advances slowly and solemnly.*)

CONDUCTOR. I trust Madame will not speak of this to the Administration. It was a pure misunderstanding. (*He salutes and runs for the train as it starts moving.*)

BURGOMASTER. (*Bows.*) Gracious lady, as Burgomaster of the town of Güllen, I have the honor— (*The rest of the speech is lost in the roar of the departing TRAIN. He continues speaking and gesturing, and at last bows amid applause as the TRAIN noises end.*)

CLAIRE. Thank you, Mr. Burgomaster. (*She glances at the beaming faces of the* MEN, *who bow in turn, and lastly at* SCHILL, *whom she does not recognize. She turns Upstage.*)

SCHILL. Clara!

CLAIRE. (*Turns and stares.*) Anton?

SCHILL. (*Moves toward her.*) Yes. It's good that you've come back, Clara—

CLAIRE. Yes. I've waited for this moment. All my life. Ever since I left Güllen.

SCHILL. (*A little embarrassed.*) That is very kind of you to say, Clara.

CLAIRE. And have you thought about me?

SCHILL. Naturally. Always. You know that.

CLAIRE. Those were happy times we spent together.

SCHILL. Unforgettable. (*He smiles reassuringly at the* BURGOMASTER.)

CLAIRE. Call me by the name you used to call me.

SCHILL. (*Whispers; he is close to her.*) My kitten.

CLAIRE. (*Backs off a step.*) What?

SCHILL. (*Louder.*) My kitten.

CLAIRE. And what else?

SCHILL. Little witch.

CLAIRE. I used to call you my black panther. You're grey now, and soft.

SCHILL. But you are still the same, little witch.

CLAIRE. I am the same? (*She laughs.*) Oh no, my black panther. I am not at all the same.

SCHILL. (*Gallantly.*) In my eyes you are. I see no difference.

CLAIRE. Would you like to meet my fiancé? Pedro Cabral. He owns an enormous plantation in Brazil.

SCHILL. A pleasure.

CLAIRE. We're to be married soon.

SCHILL. Congratulations.

CLAIRE. He will be my eighth husband. (PEDRO *stands by himself, Down Right.*) Pedro, come here and show your face. Come along, darling—come here! Don't sulk. Say hello. (PEDRO *crosses to her.*)

PEDRO. Hello.

CLAIRE. A man of few words. Isn't he charming? A diplomat. He's interested only in fishing. Isn't he handsome in his Latin way? You'd swear he was a Brazilian. But he's not—he's a Greek. His father was a white Russian. We were betrothed by a Bulgarian priest. We plan to be married in a few days here in the cathedral.

BURGOMASTER. Here in the cathedral? What an honor for us!

CLAIRE. No, it was my dream, when I was seventeen, to be married in Güllen cathedral. The dreams of youth are sacred, don't you think so, Anton?

SCHILL. Yes, of course.

CLAIRE. Yes, of course. I think so, too. Now I would like to look at the town. (*The* MIXED CHOIR *arrives from Up Left, breathless, in ordinary clothes with green sashes.*) What's all this? Go away— What's the matter with them? (*She laughs.*) Ha! Ha! Ha!

TEACHER. Dear lady— (*He steps forward, having put on a sash also.*) Dear lady, as Rector of the High School and a devotee of that noble muse—Music, I take pleasure in presenting the Güllen Mixed Choir.

CLAIRE. How do you do?

TEACHER. Who will sing for you an ancient folk song

of the region with specially amended words—if you would deign to listen.

CLAIRE. (*Sits.*) Very well. Fire away.

(*The* TEACHER *blows a "D" on his pitchpipe. The* MIXED CHOIR *begins to sing the ancient folk song with the amended words. [Words to this song will be found in back of book.] Just then the station BELL starts ringing. The song is drowned in the roar of the passing EXPRESS. [SOUND CUE # 5.] The* STATION MASTER *salutes. When the train has passed, there is applause.*)

BURGOMASTER. The church bell! The church bell! Where's the church bell? (*The* PASTOR *shrugs helplessly.*)

CLAIRE. Thank you, Professor. They sang beautifully. The little blonde bass—no, not that one—the one with the big Adam's apple—was most impressive. (*The* TEACHER *bows. The* POLICEMAN *pushes his way professionally through the* MIXED CHOIR *and comes to attention in front of* CLAIRE. Now who are you?

POLICEMAN. (*Clicks heels and salutes.*) Police Chief Schultz. At your service.

CLAIRE. (*She looks him up and down.*) I have no need of you at the moment. But I think there may be work for you by and by. Tell me, do you know how to close an eye?

POLICEMAN. How else could I get along in my profession?

CLAIRE. You might practise closing both. (POLICEMAN *bows and moves Down Left.*)

SCHILL. (*Laughs.*) What a sense of humor, eh?

BURGOMASTER. (*Puts on the top hat.*) Permit me to present my grandchildren, gracious lady. Hermine and Adolphine. There's only my wife still to come. (*He wipes the perspiration from his brow, and replaces the hat.*

The LITTLE GIRLS *present the roses with elaborate curtseys.*)

CLAIRE. Thank you, my dears. Congratulations, Burgomaster. Extraordinary children. (*She plants the roses in* PEDRO'S *arms. The* BURGOMASTER *secretly passes his top hat to the* PASTOR, *who puts it on.*)

BURGOMASTER. Our pastor, Madame. (*The* PASTOR *takes off the hat and bows. Moves to bench, takes* CLAIRE'S *hand and kisses it.*)

CLAIRE. Ah. The Pastor. How do you do? Is it you that gives consolation to the dying?

PASTOR. (*A bit puzzled.*) That is part of my ministry, yes.

CLAIRE. And to those who are condemned to death?

PASTOR. Capital punishment has been abolished in this country, Madame.

CLAIRE. I see. Well, it could be restored, I suppose. (*The* PASTOR *hands back the hat. He shrugs his shoulders in confusion.*)

SCHILL. (*Laughs.*) What an original sense of humor!

(ALL *laugh, a little blankly.*)

CLAIRE. (*Rising.*) Well, I can't sit here all day—I would like to see the town.

BURGOMASTER. (*Offers his arm.*) May I have the honor, gracious lady?

CLAIRE. Thank you, but these legs are not what they were. This one was broken in five places.

SCHILL. (*Full of concern.*) My kitten!

CLAIRE. When my airplane bumped into a mountain in Afghanistan. All the others were killed. Even the pilot. As you see, I survived. But I don't fly any more.

SCHILL. But you're as strong as ever now.

CLAIRE. Stronger.

BURGOMASTER. Never fear, gracious lady. The town doctor has a car.

CLAIRE. I never ride in motors.

BURGOMASTER. You never ride in motors?

CLAIRE. Not since my Ferrari crashed in Hong Kong.

SCHILL. But how do you travel, then, little witch? On a broom?

CLAIRE. Mike— Max. (*She claps her hands. Two huge* BODYGUARDS *come in, first bay Left, carrying a sedan chair. She sits in it.*) I travel this way—a bit antiquated of course. But perfectly safe. (BODYGUARDS *pick up chair.*) Ha! Ha! Aren't they magnificent? Mike and Max. I bought them in America. They were in jail, condemned to the chair. I had them pardoned. Now they're condemned to my chair. I paid fifty thousand dollars apiece for them. You couldn't get them now for twice the sum. The sedan chair comes from the Louvre. I fancied it so much that the President of France gave it to me. The French are so impulsive, don't you think so, Anton? Go! (MIKE *and* MAX *start to carry her off.*)

BURGOMASTER. (*Crosses in front of chair.*) You wish to visit the cathedral? And the old town hall?

CLAIRE. No. The great barn. And the forest of Konradsweil. I wish to go with Anton and visit our old haunts once again. (SCHILL *crosses to chair and takes her hand.*)

THE PASTOR. Very touching.

CLAIRE. (*To the* BUTLER.) Will you send the luggage and the coffin to The Golden Apostle.

BURGOMASTER. (*Peering around* SCHILL.) The coffin?

CLAIRE. Yes. I brought one with me. Go.

TEACHER. Hip-Hip—Hurrah!!

ALL. Hurrah! Hip-Hip, Hurrah! Hurrah!

(THEY *bear her off Up Left in the direction of the town. The* BURGOMASTER *makes a gesture. The* TOWNSPEOPLE *burst into cheers. The church* BELL *rings. SOUND CUE # 6.*)

BURGOMASTER. (*As* ALL *follow the chair off but the* POLICEMAN. [*SOUND CUE # 7. CROSS FADE # 6 UNDER.*] Ah, thank God—the bell at last!

(*The* POLICEMAN *is about to follow the others when the
two* BLIND MEN *appear from First Bay Left. They
carry guitar and mandolin case. They are not young,
yet they seem childish, a strange effect. They are
dressed exactly alike, though they are of different
height and features, and so make the effect of being
twins. They walk slowly, feeling their way. Their
voices, when they speak, are curiously high and
flute-like, and they have a curious trick of repeti-
tion.*)

FIRST BLIND MAN. We're in—
BOTH. Güllen.
FIRST BLIND MAN. We breathe—
SECOND BLIND MAN. We breathe—
BOTH BLIND MEN. We breathe the air, the air of
Güllen.
POLICEMAN. (*Startled.*) Who are you?
FIRST BLIND MAN. We belong to the lady.
SECOND BLIND MAN. We belong to the lady. She calls
us—
FIRST BLIND MAN. Kobby.
SECOND BLIND MAN. And Lobby.
POLICEMAN. (*A step toward them.*) Madame Zacha-
nassian is staying at The Golden Apostle.
FIRST BLIND MAN. We're blind.
SECOND BLIND MAN. We're blind.
POLICEMAN. Blind? Come along with me, then. I'll
take you there.
FIRST BLIND MAN. Thank you, Mr. Policeman.
SECOND BLIND MAN. Thanks very much. (*They cross
toward Center.*)
(*SOUND CUE # 7.*)
POLICEMAN. Hey! (*The* MEN *stop abruptly and turn.*)
How do you know I'm a policeman, if you're blind?
BOTH BLIND MEN. By your voice. By your voice.
FIRST BLIND MAN. All policemen sound the same.
POLICEMAN. (*Steps toward them.*) You've had a lot
to do with police, have you, little men?

FIRST BLIND MAN. Men he calls us!

BOTH BLIND MEN. Men!

POLICEMAN. What are you then?

BOTH BLIND MEN. You'll see. You'll see. (*The* POLICEMAN *claps his hands suddenly. The* MEN *turn sharply toward the sound. The* POLICEMAN *is convinced they are blind.*)

POLICEMAN. What's your trade?

BOTH BLIND MEN. We have no trade.

SECOND BLIND MAN. We play music.

FIRST BLIND MAN. We sing.

SECOND BLIND MAN. We amuse the lady.

FIRST BLIND MAN. We look after the beast.

SECOND BLIND MAN. We feed it.

FIRST BLIND MAN. We stroke it.

SECOND BLIND MAN. We take it for walks.

POLICEMAN. What beast?

BOTH BLIND MEN. You'll see—you'll see.

SECOND BLIND MAN. We give it raw meat.

FIRST BLIND MAN. And she gives us chicken and wine.

SECOND BLIND MAN. Every day—

BOTH BLIND MEN. Every day.

POLICEMAN. (*Shrugs in wonder.*) Rich people have strange tastes!

BOTH BLIND MEN. Strange tastes—strange tastes.

POLICEMAN. (*Puts on his helmet.*) Come along, I'll take you to the lady.

BOTH BLIND MEN. We know the way—we know the way. (*They turn and walk off Center between the lampposts.* [*SOUND CUE* # 8.])

(*The station and the little house vanish, Right and Left. The backdrop and the groundrows are flown out of sight. A sign descends from the flies. It reads DER GOLDENE APOSTEL. The scene dissolves into the interior of the inn.* [*See Scene Design* # 2.] *The Golden Apostle is seen to be in the last stages of decay. The walls are cracked and mouldering, and the plaster is falling from the ancient lath. A table represents the cafe of the inn. The* BURGOMASTER *and the* TEACHER *enter from Third Left and carry table Downstage to marks. A procession of* TOWNSPEOPLE *carrying many pieces of luggage passes. Then comes a coffin; lastly a panther cage covered with a canvas. They cross the stage from Left to Right. CUT SOUND.)*

BURGOMASTER. Trunks. Suitcases. Boxes. (*He looks up apprehensively at the ceiling.*) The floor will never bear the weight. (*As the large covered box is carried in, he peers under the canvas, then draws back.*) Good God!

TEACHER. Why, what's in it?

BURGOMASTER. A live panther! (*They laugh. He lifts his glass solemnly.*) Your health, Professor. Let's hope she puts the Foundry back on its feet.

TEACHER. (*Lifts his glass.*) And the Wagonworks.

BURGOMASTER. And the Golden Eagle Pencil Factory. Once that starts moving, everything else will go. Prosit. (*They touch glasses and drink.*)

TEACHER. What does she need a panther for?

BURGOMASTER. Don't ask me. The whole thing is too much for me. The Pastor had to go home and lie down.

TEACHER. (*Sets down his glass.*) If you want to know the truth, she frightens me.

BURGOMASTER. (*Nods gravely.*) She's a strange one.

TEACHER. You understand, Burgomaster, a man who for twenty-two years has been correcting the Latin compositions of the students of Güllen is not unaccustomed to surprises. I have seen things to make one's hair stand on end. But when this woman suddenly appeared on the platform, a shudder tore through me. (*Crosses Center, then to table.*) It was as though out of the clear sky all at once a fury descended upon us, beating its black wings—

POLICEMAN. (*Comes in Up Center. He mops his face.*) Ah! Now the old place is livening up a bit! (*To Down Left of table.*)

BURGOMASTER. Ah, Schultz, come and join us.

POLICEMAN. Thank you. (*He calls.*) Beer!

BURGOMASTER. Well, what's the news from the front?

POLICEMAN. (*Crosses Center.*) I'm just back from Schiller's barn. My God! What a scene! She had us all tiptoeing around in the straw as if we were in church. Nobody dared to speak above a whisper. And the way she carried on! I was so embarrassed I let them go to the forest by themselves.

BURGOMASTER. Does the fiancé go with them?

POLICEMAN. (*Nods.*) With his fishing rod and his landing net. In full marching order. (*He calls again.*) Beer!

(THIRD MAN *enters with beer First Bay Left, gives beer to* POLICEMAN, *exits Second Bay Left.*)

BURGOMASTER. But what does she expect to find in the Konradsweil forest?

POLICEMAN. The same thing she expected to find in the old barn, I suppose. The—the—

TEACHER. (*Crosses Center.*) The ashes of her youthful love.

POLICEMAN. Exactly.

TEACHER. It's poetry.

POLICEMAN. Poetry.

TEACHER. Sheer poetry! It makes one think of Shakespeare, of Wagner. Of Romeo and Juliet.

BURGOMASTER. Yes, you're right. (*Solemnly rises as they lift their glasses.*) Gentlemen, I would like to propose a toast. To our great and good friend Anton Schill, who is even now working on our behalf.

POLICEMAN. Yes! He's really working.

BURGOMASTER. Gentlemen, to the best-loved citizen of this town. My successor, Anton Schill!

(*They raise their glasses and* ALL *repeat "Anton Schill"! At this point an unearthly SCREAM is heard. [SOUND CUE # 9.] It is the black panther howling Offstage Right.*)

(The sign of the Golden Apostle rises out of sight. The LIGHTS go down. The inn vanishes. Only the wooden bench of Scene 1 is left on the stage, Down Right. [See Scene Design # 3.] The procession comes on Upstage through Fifth Bay Left. The two BODYGUARDS *carry in* CLAIRE'S *sedan chair. Next to it walks* SCHILL. PEDRO *walks behind with his fishing rod. Last come the* TWO BLIND MEN *playing mandolin and guitar and, finally, the* BUTLER. CLAIRE *alights.)*

CLAIRE. Stop! Take my chair off somewhere else. I'm tired of looking at you. *(The* BODYGUARDS *and the sedan chair go off Up Right Bay.)* Pedro darling, your brook is just a little further along down that path. Listen. You can hear it from here. Bobby, take him and show him where it is.

BLIND MEN. We'll show him the way—we'll show him the way.

(They go off Second Bay Left. PEDRO *follows.* BOBBY *walks off Up Right.)*

CLAIRE. *(Comes Downstage with* SCHILL.*)* Look, Anton. Our tree. There's the heart you carved in the bark long ago.

SCHILL. Yes. It's still there.

CLAIRE. How it has grown! The trunk is black and wrinkled. Why, its limbs are twice what they were! Some of them have died.

SCHILL. It's aged. But it's there.

CLAIRE. Like everything else. *(She crosses, examining other trees.)* Oh, how tall they are. How long it is since I walked here, barefoot over the pine needles and the damp leaves! Look, Anton. A fawn.

SCHILL. Yes, a fawn. It's the season.

CLAIRE. *(They sit together on bench.)* I thought everything would be changed. But it's all just as we left it. This is the seat we sat on years ago. Under these branches you kissed me. And over there under the hawthorn, where the moss is soft and green, we would lie in each other's arms. It is all as it used to be. Only **we** have changed.

SCHILL. Not so much, little witch. I remember the first night we spent together, you ran away and I chased you till I was quite breathless—

CLAIRE. Yes.

SCHILL. Then I was angry and started to go home, when suddenly I heard you call and I looked up, and there you were sitting in a tree laughing down at me.

CLAIRE. No. It was in the great barn. I was in the hayloft.

SCHILL. Were you?

CLAIRE. Yes. What else do you remember?

SCHILL. I remember the morning we went swimming by the waterfall, and afterwards we were lying together on the big rock in the sun when suddenly we heard footsteps and we just had time to snatch up our clothes and run behind the bushes when the old pastor appeared and scolded you for not being in school.

CLAIRE. No. It was the schoolmaster who found us. It was Sunday and I was supposed to be in church.

SCHILL. Really?

CLAIRE. Yes. Tell me more.

SCHILL. (*Turns and looks away.*) I remember the time your father beat you, and you showed me the cuts on your back, and I swore I'd kill him. And the next day I dropped a tile from a rooftop and split his head open.

CLAIRE. You missed him.

SCHILL. No!

CLAIRE. You hit old Mr. Reiner.

SCHILL. Did I?

CLAIRE. Yes. I was seventeen, And you were not yet twenty. You were so handsome. You were the best-looking boy in town.

SCHILL. And you were the prettiest girl.

CLAIRE. We were made for each other.

SCHILL. So we were.

CLAIRE. But you married Mathilde Blumhard and her store and I married old Zachanassian and his oil wells. He found me in a whorehouse in Hamburg. It was my hair that entangled him, the old golden beetle.

SCHILL. Clara!

CLAIRE. (*She claps her hands.*) Bobby! A cigar.

(BOBBY *appears Third Bay Right, with a leather case. He selects a cigar, lights it, puts it in a holder, and presents it to* CLAIRE.)

SCHILL. My kitten smokes cigars!

CLAIRE. Yes, I adore them. Would you care for one?

SCHILL. Yes, please. I've never smoked one of those.

(BOBBY *gives him a cigar, then exits Third Right.*)

CLAIRE. It's a taste I acquired from old Zachanassian. Among other things. He was a real connoisseur.

SCHILL. We used to sit on this bench once, you and I, and smoke cigarettes. Do you remember?

CLAIRE. Yes. I remember.

SCHILL. The cigarettes I bought from Mathilde.

CLAIRE. No. She gave them to you for nothing.

SCHILL. Don't be angry with me for marrying Mathilde.

CLAIRE. She had money.

SCHILL. And what a lucky thing for you that I did!

CLAIRE. Oh?

SCHILL. You were so young, so beautiful. You deserved a better fate than to be stuck in this wretched town without any future.

CLAIRE. Yes?

SCHILL. If you had stayed in Güllen and married me, your life would have been wasted like mine.

CLAIRE. Oh?

SCHILL. My God, Clara, look at me. A broken shopkeeper in a bankrupt town!

CLAIRE. But you have your family.

SCHILL. My family! Never for a moment do they let me forget my failure, my poverty.

CLAIRE. Mathilde has not made you happy?

SCHILL. (*Shrugs.*) What does it matter?

CLAIRE. And the children?

SCHILL. (*Shakes his head.*) They're so completely materialistic. You know, they have no interest whatever in higher things.

CLAIRE. How sad for you.

(*A moment's pause during which only the faint tinkling of the MUSIC is heard.*)

SCHILL. Yes. You know, since you went away my life has passed by like a stupid dream. I've hardly once been out of this town. Five days at a lake years ago. It rained all the time. A trip to Berlin, once. That's all.

CLAIRE. The world is much the same everywhere.

SCHILL. At least you've seen it.

CLAIRE. Yes. I've seen it.

SCHILL. You've lived in it.

CLAIRE. I've lived in it. The world and I have been on very intimate terms.

SCHILL. Now that you've come back, perhaps things will change.

CLAIRE. Naturally. I won't leave my native town in this condition.

SCHILL. It will take millions to put us on our feet again.

CLAIRE. I have millions.

SCHILL. One, two, three—

CLAIRE. Why not?

SCHILL. You mean—you will help us?

CLAIRE. Yes.

(*A WOODPECKER is heard in the distance.*)

SCHILL. I knew it—I knew it! I told them you were

generous, I told them you were good. Oh, my kitten! (*He takes her hand.*)

CLAIRE. (*She turns her head away and listens.*) Listen! A woodpecker.

SCHILL. It's all just the way it was in the days when we were young and full of courage. The sun high above the pines. Great white clouds, piling up on one another. [*SOUND CUE* # 12.] The cry of the cukoo in the distance. The wind rustling the leaves like the sound of surf on a beach. Just as it was years ago. If only we could roll back time and be together always.

CLAIRE. Is that your wish?

SCHILL. You left me, but you never left my heart. (*He raises her hand to his lips.*) The same soft little hand.

CLAIRE. No, not quite the same. It was crushed to a pulp in the plane accident. But they mended it. They ment everything nowadays.

SCHILL. Crushed? You wouldn't know it. (*Points.*) Another fawn.

CLAIRE. The old wood is alive with memories—

(PEDRO *appears, Second Bay Left, followed by* BLIND MEN. PEDRO *has a fish in his hand, which is dripping water.*)

PEDRO. See what I've caught, darling. See? A pike. Over two kilos.

THE TWO BLIND MEN. (*Clap their hands.*) A pike! A pike! Hurrah! Hurrah!

(CLAIRE, SCHILL *and* PEDRO *exit Right 4, followed by* BLIND MEN. *The applause is taken up on all sides. The walls of the cafe are wheeled in by* TOWNS-PEOPLE. *A BRASS BAND strikes up a march tune.* [*SOUND CUE* # 13.] *The door of the Golden Apostle descends.* TOWNSPEOPLE *bring in tables and lay them with ragged tablecloths, cracked china and glassware. Three tables are placed Center, Down*

Right and Down Left, the one in Center on a plat-
form. [See Scene Design # 4.] The PASTOR *enters*
Up Center. Other TOWNSPEOPLE *filter in Left and*
Right. THREE ATHLETES *in gymnastic costume form*
a human pyramid Down Center. The applause con-
tinues.)

BURGOMASTER. (*Runs in Up Center.*) Sing out! She's
coming! (CLAIRE *enters Up Center, followed by* BOBBY.
THE TEACHER *conducts them in same song sung earlier*
by CHOIR. *When the song ends,* ALL *applaud.*) The
applause is meant for you, gracious lady.

CLAIRE. (*At table Center.*) The band deserves it more
than I. They blow from the heart. And the human pyramid was beautiful. You—show me your muscles. (*An*
ATHLETE *kneels before her.*) Superb. Wonderful arms,
powerful hands. Have you ever strangled a man with
them?

ATHLETE. Strangled?

CLAIRE. Yes. It's perfectly simple. A little pressure in
the proper place, and the rest goes by itself. As in
politics.

(*The* BURGOMASTER'S WIFE *crosses to her, simpering.*)

BURGOMASTER. Permit me to present my wife, Madame
Zachanassian.

CLAIRE. Annette Dummermuth. The head of our class.

BURGOMASTER. (*He presents another sour-looking*
WOMAN.) Frau Schill.

CLAIRE. Mathilde Blumhard. I remember the way you
used to follow Anton with your eyes, from behind the
shop door. You've grown a little thin and dry, my poor
Mathilde.

SCHILL. (*Crosses to her with a* GIRL *and* BOY.) My
daughter Ottilie.

CLAIRE. Your daughter—

SCHILL. My son, Karl.

CLAIRE. Your son! Two of them!

(*The* TOWN DOCTOR *comes in, Up Left to Center. He is
a man of fifty, strong and stocky, with bristly black
hair, a mustache and a sabre cut on his cheek. He is
wearing an old cutaway.*)

DOCTOR. Well, well, my old Mercedes got me here in
time after all!

BURGOMASTER. (*Catches* DOCTOR *at Center.*) Doctor
Nüssler, the town physician. Madame Zachanassian.

DOCTOR. Deeply honored, Madame. (*He kisses her
hand.* CLAIRE *studies him.*)

CLAIRE. It is you who signs the death certificates?

DOCTOR. Death certificates?

CLAIRE. When someone dies.

DOCTOR. Why certainly. That is one of my duties.

CLAIRE. And when the heart dies, what do you put
down? Heart failure?

SCHILL. (*Laughing.*) What a golden sense of humor!

DOCTOR. Bit grim, wouldn't you say?

SCHILL. Not at all, not at all. (*Behind* BURGOMASTER,
whispers.) She's promised us a million.

BURGOMASTER. (*Turns his head.*) What?

SCHILL. A million!

ALL. (*Whisper.*) A million!

CLAIRE. (*Turns toward them.*) Burgomaster.

BURGOMASTER. Yes?

CLAIRE. (*Sits at table Center.*) I'm hungry. (GIRLS
and WAITER *fill glasses, bring food. General stir.* ALL
take their places at the table. BURGOMASTER, *seated next
to* CLAIRE, *opens champagne.* ALL *applaud.*) Are you
going to make a speech?

BURGOMASTER. (*He bows and rises, tapping his knife
on his glass. He is radiant with good will.* ALL *applaud.*)
Gracious lady and friends. Gracious lady, it is now many
years since you first left your native town of Güllen,
which was founded by the Elector Hasso and which
nestles in the green slope between the forest of Konradsweil and the beautiful valley of Pückenried. Much has
taken place in this time, much that is evil.

TEACHER. That's true.

BURGOMASTER. The world is not what it was; it has become harsh and bitter, and we too have had our share of harshness and bitterness. But in all this time, dear lady, we have never forgotten our little Clara. (*Applause.*) Many years ago you brightened the town with your pretty face as a child, and now once again you brighten it with your presence. (*Polite applause.*) We haven't forgotten you, and we haven't forgotten your family. Your mother, beautiful and robust even in her old age— (*He looks for his notes on the table.*) although unfortunately taken from us in the bloom of her youth by an infirmity of the lungs. Your respected father, Siegfried Wäscher, the builder, an example of whose work next to our railway station is often visited by our townspeople— (SCHILL *covers his face.*) that is to say, admired—a lasting monument to local design and local workmanship. And you, gracious lady, whom we remember as a golden-haired— (*He looks at her.*)—little red-headed sprite romping about our peaceful streets—on your way to school—which of us does not treasure your memory? (*He pokes nervously at his notebook.*) We well remember your scholarly attainments—

TEACHER. Yes.

BURGOMASTER. Natural history— Extraordinary sense of justice. And, above all, your supreme generosity. (*Great applause.*) We shall never forget how you once spent the whole of your little savings to buy a sack of potatoes for a poor starving widow who was in need of food. (*The* CHILDREN *serve wine.*) Gracious lady, ladies and gentlemen, today our little Clara has become the world-famous Claire Zachanassian who has founded hospitals, soup-kitchens, charitable institutes, art-projects, libraries, nurseries, and schools, and now that she has at last once more returned to the town of her birth, sadly fallen as it is, I say in the name of all her loving friends who have sorely missed her: Long live our Clara!

ALL. Long live our Clara!

(*Cheers and applause.* [*SOUND CUE # 14.*])

CLAIRE. (*Rises.*) Mr. Burgomaster. Fellow townsmen. I am greatly moved by the nature of your welcome and the disinterested joy which you have manifested on the occasion of my visit to my native town. I was not quite the lovely child the Burgomaster described in his gracious address.

BURGOMASTER. Too modest, Madame.

CLAIRE. In school I was beaten—

TEACHER. Not by me.

CLAIRE. And the sack of potatoes which I presented to Widow Boll, I stole with the help of Anton Schill, not to save the old trull from starvation but so that for once I might sleep with Anton in a real bed instead of under the trees of the forest. (*The* TOWNSPEOPLE *look grave, embarrassed.*) Nevertheless I shall try to deserve your good opinion. In memory of the seventeen years I spent among you, I am prepared to hand over as a gift to the town of Güllen the sum of one billion marks. Five hundred million to the town and five hundred million to be divided per capita among the citizens.

(*There is a moment of dead silence.*)

BURGOMASTER. A billion marks?

CLAIRE. On one condition. (*Sits.*)

(*Suddenly a movement of uncontrollable joy breaks out. PEOPLE jump on chairs, dance about, yell excitedly. The ATHLETES turn handsprings in front of the speaker's table.*)

SCHILL. Oh Clara, you astonishing, incredible, magnificent woman! What a heart! What a gesture! Oh—my little witch! (*He kisses her hand.*)

BURGOMASTER. (*Comes Down Center and holds up his hand for order.*) Quiet! Quiet, please! On one condition, the gracious lady said. Now, Madame, may we know what that condition is?

CLAIRE. I will tell you. In exchange for my billion marks, I want justice. (*Silence.*)

BURGOMASTER. Justice, Madame?

CLAIRE. I wish to buy justice.

BURGOMASTER. But justice cannot be bought, Madame.

CLAIRE. Everything can be bought.

BURGOMASTER. I don't understand at all.

CLAIRE. Bobby, step forward.

BOBBY. (*Crosses Center. He takes off his dark glasses and turns his face with a solemn air.*) Does anyone here present recognize me?

FRAU SCHILL. Hofer! Hofer!

ALL. Who? What's that?

TEACHER. (*Rises and takes a step toward him.*) Not Chief Magistrate Hofer, who was on the Governing Board?

BOBBY. Exactly. (TEACHER *returns to his place.*) Chief Magistrate Hofer. When Madame Zachanassian was a girl, I was presiding judge at the criminal court of Güllen. I served there until twenty-five years ago when Madame Zachanassian offered me the opportunity of entering her service as butler. I accepted. You may consider it a strange employment for a member of the magistracy, but the salary—

CLAIRE. (*Bangs mallet on table.*) Come to the point.

BOBBY. You have heard Madame Zachanassian's offer. She will give you a billion marks—when you have undone the injustice that she suffered at your hands here in Güllen as a girl. (ALL *murmur.*)

BURGOMASTER. Injustice at our hands? Impossible!

BOBBY. Anton Schill—

SCHILL. Yes?

BOBBY. Kindly stand.

SCHILL. (*Rises. He smiles, as if puzzled. He shrugs.*) Yes?

BOBBY. In those days, a bastardy case was tried before me. Madame Claire Zachanassian, at that time called

Clara Wäscher, charged you with being the father of her illegitimate child. (*Silence.*) You denied the charge. And produced two witnesses in your support.

SCHILL. That's ancient history. An absurd business. We were children. Who remembers?

CLAIRE. Where are the blind men?

THE TWO BLIND MEN. (*Enter from First Bay Right.*) Here we are. Here we are. (MIKE and MAX *push them forward to below Right table.*)

BOBBY. You recognize these men, Anton Schill?

SCHILL. (*Steps toward them.*) I never saw them before in my life. What are they?

THE TWO BLIND MEN. We've changed. We've changed.

BOBBY. What were your names in your former life?

FIRST BLIND MAN. I was Jacob Hueblein. Jacob Hueblein.

SECOND BLIND MAN. I was Ludwig Sparr. Ludwig Sparr.

BOBBY. (*To* SCHILL.) Well?

SCHILL. These names mean nothing to me.

BOBBY. Jacob Hueblein and Ludwig Sparr, do you recognize the defendant?

FIRST BLIND MAN. We're blind.

SECOND BLIND MAN. We're blind.

SCHILL. Ha-ha-ha!

BOBBY. By his voice?

TWO BLIND MEN. By his voice. By his voice.

BOBBY. At that trial, I was the judge. And you?

TWO BLIND MEN. We were the witnesses.

BOBBY. And what did you testify on that occasion?

FIRST BLIND MAN. That we had slept with Clara Wäscher.

SECOND BLIND MAN. Both of us. Many times.

BOBBY. And was it true?

FIRST BLIND MAN. No.

SECOND BLIND MAN. We swore falsely.

BOBBY. And why did you swear falsely?

FIRST BLIND MAN. Anton Schill bribed us.

SECOND BLIND MAN. He bribed us.

BOBBY. With what?

BOTH. With a bottle of schnapps.

BOBBY. And now tell the people what happened to you. (*They hesitate and whimper.*) Speak!

FIRST BLIND MAN. (*In a low voice.*) She tracked us down.

BOBBY. Madame Zachanassian tracked them down. Jacob Hueblein was found in Canada. Ludwig Sparr in Australia. And when she found you, what did she do to you?

SECOND BLIND MAN. She handed us over to Mike and Max.

BOBBY. And what did Mike and Max do to you?

FIRST BLIND MAN. (*Covering his face.*) They made us what you see. (*They cover their faces.* MIKE *and* MAX *push them off First Bay Right.*)

BOBBY. And there you have it. We are all present in Güllen once again. The plaintiff. The defendant. The two false witnesses. The judge. Many years have passed. Does the plaintiff have anything further to add?

CLAIRE. There is nothing to add.

BOBBY. And the defendant?

SCHILL. (*Crosses and kneels to* CLAIRE.) Why are you doing this? It was all dead and buried.

BOBBY. What happened to the child that was born?

CLAIRE. (*In low voice.*) It lived a year.

BOBBY. And what happened to you?

CLAIRE. I became a whore.

BOBBY. Why?

CLAIRE. The judgment of the court left me no alternative. No one would trust me—no one would give me work.

BOBBY. So. And now, what is the nature of the reparation you demand?

CLAIRE. I want the life of Anton Schill.

(SCHILL *rises. His wife and children rush to him. He*

pushes them away and moves around Left table to Down Left.)

FRAU SCHILL. Anton! No! No!

SCHILL. No— No— She's joking. That happened long ago. That's all forgotten.

CLAIRE. Nothing is forgotten. Neither the mornings in the forest, nor the nights in the great barn, nor the bedroom in the cottage, nor your treachery at the end. You said this morning you wished that time might be rolled back. Very well—I have rolled it back. And now it is I who will buy justice. You bought it with a bottle of schnapps. I am willing to pay one billion marks.

BURGOMASTER. (*Stands up, very solemn and dignified.*) Madame Zachanassian, we are not in the jungle. We are in Europe. We may be poor but we are not heathens. In the name of the town of Güllen, I decline your offer. In the name of humanity. We shall never accept.

(Al l *applaud wildly. The applause turns into a sinister rhythmic beat. As* CLAIRE *rises, it dies away. She looks at the crowd, then at the* BURGOMASTER.)

CLAIRE. Thank you, Burgomaster. (*She stares at him a long moment.*) I can wait. (*Turns and exits Up Center.*)

CURTAIN

ACT TWO

SCENE: *Bring front lights Up as curtain reaches head
high. The façade of the Golden Apostle with a balcony on which chairs and a table are set out. To the
Right of the inn is a sign which reads ANTON
SCHILL, HANDLUNG. Under the sign the shop is
represented by a broken counter. Behind the counter,
some shelves with tobacco, cigarettes and liquor
bottles. Two milk cans. The shop door is imaginary,
but each entrance is indicated by a door bell with a
tinny sound. [See Scene Design # 5.]*

AT RISE: *It is early morning. SCHILL is sweeping the
shop. The SON has a pan and brush and also sweeps.
The DAUGHTER is dusting. ALL are singing "The
Happy Wanderer," as the CURTAIN rises. [Words
to this will be found in back of book.]*

SCHILL. Karl—

(KARL *crosses with a dustpan.* SCHILL *sweeps dust into
the pan. The door bell rings. The* THIRD MAN *enters
Third Bay Right, carrying a crate of eggs.*)

THIRD MAN. (*Crosses to* SCHILL, *Center.*) Morning.

SCHILL. Ah, good morning, Wechsler. You're early.

THIRD MAN. Twelve dozen eggs, medium brown.
Right?

SCHILL. Take them, Karl. (KARL *puts the crate in a
corner, Fourth Bay Left.*) Did they deliver the milk yet?
(*Moving to counter.*)

SON. Before you came down.

THIRD MAN. (*Crossing to counter.*) Eggs are going up
again, Herr Schill. First of the month. (*He gives* SCHILL
a slip to sign.)

SCHILL. What? Again? And who's going to buy them?

39

THIRD MAN. Fifty pfennig a dozen.

SCHILL. I'll have to cancel my order, that's all.

THIRD MAN. That's up to you, Herr Schill.

SCHILL. (*Signs the slip.*) There's nothing else to do. (*He hands back the slip.*) And how's the family?

THIRD MAN. (*Starts to exit.*) Oh, scraping along. Maybe now things will get better.

SCHILL. Maybe.

THIRD MAN. (*Going, Fourth Bay Right.*) Morning.

SCHILL. Karl, close the door. Don't let the flies in. (*The* CHILDREN *resume their singing.* SCHILL *crosses and sits front of counter.*) Now, listen to me, children. I have a little piece of good news for you. I didn't mean to speak of it yet a while but well, why not? Who do you suppose is going to be the next burgomaster? Eh? (*They look up at him.*) Yes, in spite of everything. It's settled. It's official. What an honor for the family, eh? Especially at a time like this. To say nothing of the salary and the rest of it.

SON. (*With slow realization, runs to* SCHILL.) Burgomaster!

SCHILL. Burgomaster. (*The* SON *shakes him warmly by the hand. The* DAUGHTER *kisses him.*) You see, you don't have to be entirely ashamed of your father. (*Silence.*) Is your mother coming down soon?

DAUGHTER. Mother's tired. She's going to stay upstairs.

SCHILL. You have a good mother, at least. There you are lucky. Oh, well, if she wants to rest, let her rest. We'll have breakfast together, the three of us. I'll fry some eggs and open a tin of the American ham. This morning we're going to breakfast like kings. (*Crosses to ladder, First Bay Left.*)

SON. (*Goes to him.*) I'd like to, only—I can't.

SCHILL. You've got to eat, you know.

SON. I've got to run down to the station. One of the laborers is sick. They said they could use me.

SCHILL. You want to work on the rails in all this heat? That's no work for a son of mine.

SON. Look, Father, we can use the money.

SCHILL. Well, if you feel you have to. (*The* SON *crosses to First Bay Right with dustpan and brush.*)

DAUGHTER. (*Crosses to* SCHILL.) I'm sorry, Father, I have to go too.

SCHILL. You too? And where is the young lady going, if I may be so bold?

DAUGHTER. There may be something for me at the employment agency.

SCHILL. Employment agency?

DAUGHTER. It's important to get there early.

(*SOUND CUE # 15.*)

SCHILL. All right. I'll have something nice for you when you get home.

SON *and* DAUGHTER. (*Salute.*) Good day, Burgomaster. (SON *and* DAUGHTER *go out Fourth Bay Right.*)

(*The* FIRST MAN *comes into* SCHILL'S *shop. Mandolin and guitar MUSIC sounds Offstage.*)

SCHILL. Good morning, Hofbauer.

FIRST MAN. (*Crossing to counter.*) Cigarettes. (SCHILL *takes a pack from the shelf.*) Not those. I'll have the green today.

SCHILL. They cost more. (*He serves him.*)

FIRST MAN. Put it in the book.

SCHILL. What?

FIRST MAN. Charge it.

SCHILL. Well, all right, I'll make an exception this time—seeing it's you, Hofbauer. (*Writes in his cash book.*)

FIRST MAN. (*Opening the pack of cigarettes as he crosses to bench and sits.*) Who's that playing out there?

SCHILL. The two blind men.

FIRST MAN. They play well.

SCHILL. To hell with them.

FIRST MAN. They make you nervous? (SCHILL *shrugs.*

The FIRST MAN *lights a cigarette.*) She's getting ready for the wedding, I hear.

SCHILL. Yes. So they say.

(*Enter* FIRST *and* SECOND WOMAN *from Fourth Bay Right. They cross to the counter.*)

FIRST WOMAN. Good morning, good morning.

SECOND WOMAN. Good morning.

FIRST MAN. Good morning.

SCHILL. Good morning, ladies.

FIRST WOMAN. Good morning, Herr Schill!

SECOND WOMAN. Good morning.

FIRST WOMAN. Milk please, Herr Schill!

SCHILL. Milk.

SECOND WOMAN. And milk for me too.

SCHILL. A litre of milk each. Right away.

FIRST WOMAN. Whole milk, please, Herr Schill!

SCHILL. Whole milk?

SECOND WOMAN. Yes. Whole milk, please.

SCHILL. Whole milk, I can only give you half a litre each of whole milk.

FIRST WOMAN. All right.

SCHILL. Half a litre of whole milk here, and half a litre of whole milk here. There you are. (*Puts milk cans in Second Bay Left.*)

FIRST WOMAN. And butter please, a quarter kilo.

SCHILL. Butter, I haven't any butter. (*Returning.*) I can give you some very nice lard?

FIRST WOMAN. No. Butter.

SCHILL. Goose fat? (FIRST WOMAN *shakes her head.*) Chicken fat?

FIRST WOMAN. Butter.

SCHILL. Butter. (*Climbs ladder Down Left.*) Now, wait a minute, though. I have a tin of imported butter here somewhere. Ah. There you are. (*Comes back behind counter with butter.*) No, sorry, she asked first, but I can order some for you from Kalberstadt tomorrow.

SECOND WOMAN. And white bread.

SCHILL. White bread. (*He takes a loaf and a knife.*)

SECOND WOMAN. The whole loaf.

SCHILL. But a whole loaf would cost—

SECOND WOMAN. Charge it. (*Holds bag open.* SCHILL *drops bread into bag.*)

SCHILL. Charge it?

FIRST WOMAN. And a package of milk chocolate.

SCHILL. Package of milk chocolate—right away.

SECOND WOMAN. One for me too, Herr Schill!

SCHILL. And a package of milk chocolate for you, too.

FIRST WOMAN. (*Moves toward chairs Up Left.*) We'll eat it here if you don't mind.

SCHILL. Yes, please do.

SECOND WOMAN. (*Follows* FIRST WOMAN *Up.*) It's so cool at the back of the shop.

SCHILL. Charge it?

WOMEN. (*They sit.*) Of course.

SCHILL. All for one, one for all.

(*Enter* SECOND MAN, *hitting shop bell.*)

SECOND MAN. (*Crossing to counter.*) Good morning.

THE TWO WOMEN. Good morning.

SCHILL. Good morning, Helmsberger.

SECOND MAN. It's going to be a hot day.

SCHILL. Phew!

SECOND MAN. How's business?

SCHILL. Fabulous. For a while no one came and now all of a sudden I'm running a luxury trade. (*Moves to Down Center.*)

SECOND MAN. Good!

SCHILL. Oh, I'll never forget the way you all stood by me at The Golden Apostle in spite of your need, in spite of everything. (*Goes to Fourth Bay Right, shakes duster and returns Center.*) That was the finest hour of my life.

FIRST MAN. We're not heathens, you know.

SECOND MAN. We're behind you, my boy; the whole town's behind you.

FIRST MAN. As firm as a rock.

FIRST WOMAN. (*Munching her chocolate.*) As firm as a rock, Herr Schill.

BOTH WOMEN. As firm as a rock.

SECOND MAN. There's no denying it—you're the most popular man in town.

FIRST MAN. (*Crosses back to Center.*) The most important.

(*SOUND CUE # 16.*)

SECOND MAN. And in the spring, God willing, you will be our Burgomaster. (*Crosses Upstage of* FIRST MAN.)

FIRST MAN. Sure as a gun.

ALL. Sure as a gun.

(*Enter* PEDRO, *Right 4, with fishing equipment and a fish in his landing net.* WOMEN *rise.*)

PEDRO. Would you please weigh my fish for me?

(*While* SCHILL *weighs fish,* PEDRO *walks around inspecting shop. He is closely followed by* FIRST *and* SECOND MEN, *who inspect him curiously.*)

SCHILL. (*Weighs it.*) Two kilos.

PEDRO. Is that all?

SCHILL. Two kilos exactly.

PEDRO. Two kilos! (*Gives* SCHILL *a tip and exits Right 4, hitting shop bell.*)

SECOND WOMAN. (*As they step down.*) The fiancé.

FIRST WOMAN. They're to be married this week. It will be a tremendous wedding.

SECOND WOMAN. I saw his picture in the paper.

FIRST WOMAN. (*Sighs.*) Ah, what a man!

SECOND MAN. (*Moves to counter.*) Give me a schnapps.

SCHILL. The usual?

SECOND MAN. No, cognac.

SCHILL. Cognac? But cognac costs twenty-two marks fifty.

SECOND MAN. We all have to splurge a little now and again—

SCHILL. Here you are. Three Star.

SECOND MAN. And a package of pipe tobacco.

SCHILL. Black or blond?

SECOND MAN. English.

SCHILL. English! But that makes twenty-three marks eighty.

SECOND MAN. Chalk it up.

SCHILL. Now look. I'll make an exception this week. Only you will have to pay me the moment your unemployment check comes in. I don't want to be kept waiting. (*Suddenly.*) Helmsberger, are those new shoes you're wearing?

SECOND MAN. (*Crosses Left of bench.* SCHILL *follows.*) Yes, what about it?

SCHILL. You too, Hofbauer. Yellow shoes! Brand new!

FIRST MAN. (*Swings legs over bench.*) So?

SCHILL. (*To the* WOMEN, *who move down.*) And you. You all have new shoes! New shoes!

FIRST WOMAN. A person can't walk around forever in the same old shoes.

SECOND WOMAN. Shoes wear out.

SCHILL. (*At Center.*) And the money. Where does the money come from?

FIRST WOMAN. We got them on credit, Herr Schill.

SECOND WOMAN. On credit.

SCHILL. On credit? And where all of a sudden do you get credit?

SECOND MAN. Everybody gives credit now.

FIRST WOMAN. You gave us credit yourself.

SCHILL. And what are you going to pay with? Eh? (*They are all silent.* SCHILL *advances upon them threateningly.*) With what? Eh? With what? With what? (*Suddenly he understands. He takes his apron off quickly, flings it on the counter, gets his jacket, and walks off with an air of determination.*)

(Now the shop sign vanishes. The shelves are pushed off. The LIGHTS go up on the balcony of The Golden Apostle, and the balcony unit itself moves forward into the optical center. [See Scene Design # 6.] CLAIRE and BOBBY step out on the balcony. CLAIRE sits down. BOBBY serves coffee. [SOUND CUE # 17.]

CLAIRE. A lovely autumn morning. A silver haze on the streets and a violet sky above. Count Holk would have liked this. Remember him, Bobby? My third husband?

BOBBY. Yes, Madame.

CLAIRE. Horrible man!

BOBBY. Yes, Madame.

CLAIRE. Where is Monsieur Pedro? Is he up yet?

BOBBY. Yes, Madame. He's fishing.

CLAIRE. Already? What a singular passion!

PEDRO. (*Comes in with the fish.*) Good morning, my love.

CLAIRE. Pedro! There you are.

PEDRO Look, my darling. Four kilos!

CLAIRE. A jewel! I'll have it grilled for your lunch. Give it to Bobby.

(PEDRO *gives fish to* BOBBY, *who exits.*)

PEDRO. (*Sits Right.*) Ah—it is so wonderful here! I like your little town.

CLAIRE. Oh, do you?

PEDRO. Yes. These people, they are all so—what is the word?

CLAIRE. Simple, honest, hardworking, decent.

PEDRO. But, my angel, you are a mind reader. That's just what I was going to say—however did you guess?

CLAIRE. I know them.

PEDRO. Yet when we arrived it was all so dirty, so—what is the word?

CLAIRE. Shabby.

PEDRO. Exactly. But now everywhere you go, you see them busy as bees, cleaning their streets—

CLAIRE. Repairing their houses, sweeping—dusting—hanging new curtains in the windows—singing as they work.

PEDRO. But you astonishing, wonderful woman! You can't see all that from here.

CLAIRE. I know them. And in their gardens— I am sure that in their gardens they are manuring the soil for the spring.

PEDRO. My angel, you know everything. This morning on my way fishing I said to myself, look at them all manuring their gardens. It is extraordinary—and it's all because of you. Your return has given them a new—what is the word?

CLAIRE. Lease on life?

PEDRO. Precisely.

CLAIRE. The town was dying, it's true. But a town doesn't have to die. I think they realize that now. People die, not towns. Bobby! (BOBBY *appears with cigar already lit.*) [*SOUND CUE* # 18.] A cigar.

(*The LIGHTS fade on the balcony which moves back Upstage, somewhat to the Right. A sign descends from the flies. It reads POLIZEI. The* POLICEMAN *pushes a desk under it. This, with the bench, becomes the police station.* [*See Scene Design* # 7.] *He places a bottle of beer and a glass on the desk and goes to hang up his coat Offstage. The TELE-PHONE rings.*)

POLICEMAN. (*On phone.*) Schultz speaking. Yes, we have a couple of rooms for the night. No, not for rent. This is not the hotel. This is the Güllen police station. (*He laughs and hangs up.* SCHILL *comes in Up Center. He is evidently nervous.*)

SCHILL. (*Crosses to desk.*) Schultz.

POLICEMAN. Hello, Schill. Come in. Sit down. Beer? (*Offers bottle from desk.*)

SCHILL. (*Sits Right end of bench.*) Thanks. (*He drinks thirstily.*)

POLICEMAN. What can I do for you?

SCHILL. I want you to arrest Madame Zachanassian.

POLICEMAN. Eh?

SCHILL. I said I want you to arrest Madame Zachanassian.

POLICEMAN. What the hell are you talking about?

SCHILL. I ask you to arrest this woman at once.

POLICEMAN. What offense has the lady committed?

SCHILL. You know perfectly well. She offered the town a billion marks—

POLICEMAN. And you want her arrested for that? (*He pours beer into his glass.*)

SCHILL. Schultz! It's your duty.

SCHULTZ. Extraordinary! Extraordinary idea! (*He drinks his beer.*)

SCHILL. I'm speaking to you as your next burgomaster.

POLICEMAN. Schill, that's true. The lady offered us a billion marks. But that doesn't entitle us to take police action against her.

SCHILL. Why not?

POLICEMAN. In order to be arrested, a person must first commit a crime.

SCHILL. Incitement to murder.

POLICEMAN. Incitement to murder is a crime. I agree.

SCHILL. Well?

POLICEMAN. And such a proposal—if serious—constitutes an assault.

SCHILL. That's what I mean.

POLICEMAN. But her offer can't be serious.

SCHILL. Why?

POLICEMAN. The price is much too high. In a case like yours, one offers a thousand marks, at the most two thousand. But not a billion! That's ridiculous. And even if she meant it, that would only prove she was out of her mind. And that's not a matter for the police.

SCHILL. Whether she's out of her mind or not, the danger to me is the same. That's obvious.

POLICEMAN. Look Schill, you show us where anyone threatens your life in any way—say, for instance, a man points a gun at you—and we'll be there in a flash.

SCHILL. (*Gets up, crosses Center.*) So I'm to wait till someone points a gun at me?

POLICEMAN. Pull yourself together, Schill. We're all for you in this town.

SCHILL. I wish I could believe it.

POLICEMAN. You don't believe it?

SCHILL. No. No, I don't. (*Turns to look at* POLICE-MAN.) All of a sudden my customers are buying white bread, whole milk, butter, imported tobacco. What does it mean?

POLICEMAN. It means business is picking up.

(*SOUND CUE # 19.*)

SCHILL. (*Crosses back to desk.*) Helmsberger lives on the dole; he hasn't earned anything in five years. Today he bought French cognac.

POLICEMAN. I'll have to try your cognac one of these days.

SCHILL. (*Crosses Center.*) And shoes. They all have new shoes.

POLICEMAN. And what have you got against new shoes? I'm wearing a new pair myself. (*He holds out his legs, placing them on bench.*)

SCHILL. You too?

POLICEMAN. Why not? (*He pours out the rest of his beer.*)

SCHILL. Is that Pilsener you're drinking now?

POLICEMAN. It's the only thing.

SCHILL. You used to drink the local brew.

POLICEMAN. Hogwash.

SCHILL. Listen. You hear?

POLICEMAN. "The Merry Widow." Yes.

SCHILL. No. It's a radio.

POLICEMAN. That's Bergholzer's radio.

SCHILL. Bergholzer!

POLICEMAN. You're right. He should close his window when he plays it. I'll make a note to speak to him. (*He makes a note in his notebook.*)

SCHILL. And how can Bergholzer pay for a radio?

POLICEMAN. That's his business.

SCHILL. And you, Schultz, with your new shoes and your imported beer—how are you going to pay for them?

POLICEMAN. That's my business. (*His TELEPHONE rings. He picks it up. Moves around desk during phone conversation.*) Police Station, Güllen. What? What? Where? *Where?* How? Right, we'll deal with it. (*Hangs up.*)

SCHILL. (*He speaks during this telephone conversation. Paces up and down.*) Schultz, listen. No. Schultz, please —listen to me. Don't you see they're all— Listen, please. Look, Schultz. They're all running up debts. And out of these debts comes this sudden prosperity. (*Grabs* POLICEMAN.) And out of this prosperity comes the absolute need to kill me.

POLICEMAN. (*Putting on his jacket.*) You're imagining things.

SCHILL. (*Crosses Center.*) All she has to do is to sit on her balcony and wait.

POLICEMAN. Don't be a child.

SCHILL. You're all waiting.

POLICEMAN. Look, Schill, you can relax. (*Crosses* SCHILL *to Center.*) The police are here for your protection. They know their job. Let anyone, any time, make the slightest threat to your life, and all you have to do is let us know. We'll do the rest. . . . Now don't worry. (*Gets rifle Fourth Bay Left.*)

SCHILL. (*Sits bench.*) No, I won't.

POLICEMAN. (*Standing over* SCHILL.) And don't upset yourself. All right?

SCHILL. No. I won't. (*Then suddenly, in a low tone.*) You have a new gold tooth in your mouth!

POLICEMAN. What are you talking about?

SCHILL. (*Rises, taking* POLICEMAN'S *head in his hands, and forcing his lips open.*) A brand new, shining, gold tooth.

POLICEMAN. (*Breaks away and involuntarily levels the gun at him.*) Are you crazy? Look, I've no time to waste. Madame Zachanassian's panther's broken loose.

SCHILL. Panther?

POLICEMAN. Yes, it's at large. I've got to hunt it down.

SCHILL. You're not hunting a panther and you know it. It's me you're hunting!

(SCHULTZ *clicks on the safety and lowers the gun.*)

POLICEMAN. Schill! take my advice. Go home. Lock the door. Keep out of everyone's way. That way you'll be safe. Cheer up! Good times are just around the corner!

(*SOUND CUE* # 20. *The LIGHTS dim in this area and light up balcony.* [*See Scene Design* # 8.] PEDRO *is lounging in a chair.* CLAIRE *is smoking.*)

PEDRO. Oh, this little town oppresses me.

CLAIRE. Oh, does it? So you've changed your mind?

PEDRO. It is true, I find it charming, delightful—

CLAIRE. Picturesque.

PEDRO. Yes. After all, it's the place where you were born. But it is too quiet for me. Too provincial. Too much like all small towns everywhere. These people—look at them. They fear nothing, they desire nothing, they strive for nothing. They have everything they want. They are asleep.

CLAIRE. Perhaps one day they will come to life again.

PEDRO. My God—do I have to wait for that?

CLAIRE. Yes, you do. Why don't you go back to your fishing?

PEDRO. I think I will. (*Rises and exits.*)

CLAIRE. Pedro.

PEDRO. (*Re-enters.*) Yes, my love?

CLAIRE. Telephone the President of Hambro's Bank.

Ask him to transfer a billion marks to my current account.

PEDRO. A billion? Yes, my love. (*He goes.*)

(*LIGHTS fade on the balcony. [SOUND CUE # 21.]
A sign is flown in. It reads: RATHAUS. The counter
of SCHILL's shop is transformed into the BURGO-
MASTER's office. [See Scene Design # 9.] The
BURGOMASTER comes in Third Bay Left. He takes a
revolver from his pocket, examines it and sets it
down on the desk. As he sits down and starts smoking, SCHILL knocks.*)

BURGOMASTER. Come in.

SCHILL. (*Enters First Bay Right.*) I must have a word with you, Burgomaster.

BURGOMASTER. Ah, Schill. Sit down, my friend.

SCHILL. (*Leans on counter.*) Man to man. As your successor.

BURGOMASTER. But of course. Naturally.

SCHILL. (*Looks at the revolver.*) Is that a gun?

BURGOMASTER. Madame Zachanassian's black pan-
ther's broken loose. It's been seen near the cathedral. It's as well to be prepared.

SCHILL. Oh, yes. Of course.

BURGOMASTER. I've sent out a call for all able-bodied men with firearms. The streets have been cleared. The children have been kept in school, we don't want any accidents.

SCHILL. (*Suspiciously.*) You're making quite a thing of it.

BURGOMASTER. (*Shrugs.*) Naturally. A panther is a dangerous beast. Well? What's on your mind? Speak out. We're old friends.

SCHILL. (*Moves Upstage of counter.*) That's a good cigar you're smoking.

BURGOMASTER. Yes. Havana.

SCHILL. You used to smoke something else.

BURGOMASTER. Fortuna.

SCHILL. Cheaper.

BURGOMASTER. Too strong.

SCHILL. (*Moves around behind chair.*) A new tie? Silk?

BURGOMASTER. Yes. Do you like it?

SCHILL. And have you also bought new shoes?

BURGOMASTER. (*Brings his feet out from under the desk.*) Why, yes. I ordered a new pair from Kalberstadt. Extraordinary! However did you guess?

SCHILL. (*Moves to front of counter.*) That's why I'm here.

(*The* THIRD MAN *knocks, enters First Bay Right with typewriter.*)

BURGOMASTER. Come in.

THIRD MAN. The new typewriter, sir.

BURGOMASTER. Put it on the desk. (*The* THIRD MAN *sets it down and exits Second Bay Right.*) What's the matter with you? My dear fellow, aren't you well?

SCHILL. It's you who don't seem well, Burgomaster.

BURGOMASTER. What do you mean?

SCHILL. You look pale.

BURGOMASTER. I?

SCHILL. Your hands are trembling. (*The* BURGOMASTER *involuntarily hides his hands.*) Are you frightened?

BURGOMASTER. What have I to be afraid of?

SCHILL. Perhaps this sudden prosperity alarms you.

BURGOMASTER. Is prosperity a crime?

SCHILL. That depends on how you pay for it.

BURGOMASTER. You'll have to forgive me, Schill, but I really haven't the slightest idea what you're talking about. Am I supposed to feel like a criminal every time I order a new typewriter?

SCHILL. Do you?

BURGOMASTER. Well, I hope we haven't come here to talk about the new typewriter. Now, what was it you wanted?

SCHILL. (*Gets chair from Up Left, brings it down and*

sits across from desk.) I have come to claim the protection of the authorities.

BURGOMASTER. Against whom?

SCHILL. You know against whom.

BURGOMASTER. You don't trust us?

SCHILL. That woman has put a price on my head.

BURGOMASTER. If you don't feel safe, why don't you go to the police?

SCHILL. I've just come from the police.

BURGOMASTER. And?

SCHILL. The chief has a new gold tooth in his head.

BURGOMASTER. (*Rises and moves Center.*) A new——? Oh, Schill, really! You're forgetting. This is Güllen, the town of humane traditions. Goethe slept here. Brahms composed a quartet. You must have faith in us. This is a law-abiding community.

SCHILL. (*Rises.*) Then arrest this woman who wants to have me killed.

BURGOMASTER. Look here, Schill. God knows the lady has every right to be angry with you. What you did there wasn't very pretty. You forced two decent lads to perjure themselves and had a young girl thrown out on the streets.

SCHILL. (*Crosses and sits in* BURGOMASTER'S *chair.*) That young girl owns half the world.

(*A moment's silence.*)

BURGOMASTER. (*Leans on back of* SCHILL'S *chair.*) Very well, then, we'll speak frankly.

SCHILL. That's why I'm here.

BURGOMASTER. Man to man, just as you said. (*He clears his throat.*) Now—after what you did, you have no moral right to say a word against this lady. And I advise you not to try. Also—I regret to have to tell you this—there is no longer any question of your being elected Burgomaster.

SCHILL. Is that official?

BURGOMASTER. Official.

SCHILL. I see.

BURGOMASTER. (*Sits on counter.*) The man who is chosen to exercise the high post of Burgomaster must have, obviously, certain moral qualifications. Qualifications which, unhappily, you no longer possess. Naturally, you may count on the esteem and friendship of the town just as before. That goes without saying. The best thing will be to spread the mantle of silence over the whole miserable business.

SCHILL. So I'm to remain silent while they arrange my murder?

BURGOMASTER. (*Suddenly noble, moving Center.*) Now, who is arranging your murder? Give me the names and I will investigate the case at once. Unrelentingly. (*Moves back to counter.*) Well? The names?

SCHILL. (*Rises.*) You.

BURGOMASTER. I resent this. Do you think we want to kill you for money?

SCHILL. (*Moves around counter to him.*) No. You don't want to kill me. But you want to have me killed.

(*The LIGHTS go down.* [*SOUND CUE # 21A.*] *The stage is filled with* MEN *prowling about with rifles, as if they were stalking a quarry. In the interval the* POLICEMAN'S *bench and the* BURGOMASTER'S *desk are shifted somewhat so that they will compose the setting for the sacristy.* [*See Scene Design # 10.*] *The stage empties. The LIGHTS come up on balcony.* CLAIRE *appears.*)

CLAIRE. (*At rail,* BOBBY *enters.*) Bobby, what's going on here? What are all these men doing with guns? Whom are they hunting?

BOBBY. The black panther has escaped, Madame.

CLAIRE. Who let him out?

BOBBY. Kobby and Lobby, Madame.

CLAIRE. How excited they are! There may be shooting?

BOBBY. It is possible, Madame.

(*The LIGHTS fade on the balcony.* [*SOUND CUE #
22.*] *The* SACRISTAN *comes in. He arranges the set,
and puts the altar cloth on the altar. Then* SCHILL
comes on. He is looking for the PASTOR. *The* PASTOR
*enters, Left. He is wearing his gown and carrying a
rifle.*)

SCHILL. Sorry to disturb you, Pastor.

PASTOR. God's house is open to all. (*He sees* SCHILL *is
staring at the gun. Crosses to bench.*) Oh, the gun? That's
because of the panther. It's best to be prepared.

SCHILL. Pastor, will you help me?

PASTOR. Of course. Sit down. (*He puts the rifle on the
bench.*) What's the trouble?

SCHILL. (*Sits on the bench.*) I'm frightened.

PASTOR. (*Facing him.*) Frightened? Of what?

SCHILL. Of everyone. They're hunting me down like a
beast.

PASTOR. Have no fear of man, Schill. Fear God. Fear
not the death of the body. Fear the death of the soul.
Zip up my gown behind, Sacristan. (SACRISTAN *crosses
to him, zips him up, then returns to Upstage end of
altar.*)

SCHILL. I'm afraid, Pastor.

PASTOR. Put your trust in heaven, my friend.

SCHILL. You see, I'm not well. I shake. I have such
pains around the heart. I sweat.

PASTOR. I know. You're passing through a profound
psychic experience.

SCHILL. I'm going through hell.

PASTOR. (*Moves behind* SCHILL.) The hell you are
going through exists only within yourself. Many years
ago you betrayed a girl shamefully, for money. Now you
think that we shall sell you just as you sold her. No, my
friend, you are projecting your guilt upon others. It's
quite natural. But remember, the root of our torment lies
always within ourselves, in our hearts, in our sins. When
you have understood this, you can conquer the fears that

oppress you; you have weapons with which to destroy
them.

SCHILL. (*Turning.*) No—don't you see? Siemethofer
has bought a new washing machine.

PASTOR. Don't worry about the washing machine.
Worry about your immortal soul.

SCHILL. Stockers has a television set.

PASTOR. There is also great comfort in prayer.
Sacristan, the bands. (SCHILL *crosses to altar and kneels.
The* SACRISTAN *ties on the* PASTOR'S *bands, then crosses
to bench.* PASTOR *crosses to* SCHILL *at altar.*) Examine
your conscience, Schill. Repent. Otherwise your fears
will consume you. Believe me, this is the only way. We
have no other. (*The church BELL begins to peal.
[SOUND CUE # 23.]* SCHILL *seems relieved.*) Now I
must leave you. I have a baptism. You may stay as long
as you like. (*Crosses Center.*) Sacristan, the Bible, Liturgy and Psalter. The child is beginning to cry. I can
hear it from here. It is frightened. (SACRISTAN *gets books
from bench.*) Let us make haste to give it the only
security which this world affords.

SCHILL. A new bell?

PASTOR. Yes, its tone is marvellous, don't you think?
Full. Sonorous.

SCHILL. (*Rises, steps back in horror.*) A new bell! You
too, Pastor? You too?

PASTOR. (*He clasps his hands in horror. Then he takes*
SCHILL *into his arms.*) Oh, God, God, forgive me. We
are poor weak things, all of us. Do not tempt us further
into the hell in which you are burning. Go, Schill, my
friend, go, my brother, go while there is time.

(*The* PASTOR *goes.* SCHILL *picks up the rifle with a
gesture of desperation. He goes out with it, First
Left. As the LIGHTS fade,* MEN *appear with guns.
Two SHOTS are fired in the darkness. The LIGHTS
come up on the balcony, which moves forward. [See
Scene Design # 11.]*)

CLAIRE. Bobby! (BOBBY *enters.*) What was that shooting? Have they caught the panther?

BOBBY. He is dead, Madame.

CLAIRE. There were two shots.

BOBBY. The panther is dead, Madame.

CLAIRE. I loved him. (*Waves* BOBBY *away, and he exits.* CLAIRE *sits.*) I shall miss him.

(*The* TEACHER *comes in Fourth Bay Left, with little* GIRLS, *singing. They stop under the balcony.* [*Words for this song will be found in back of book.*]

TEACHER. Gracious lady, be so good as to accept our heartfelt condolences. Your beautiful panther is no more. Believe me, we are deeply pained that so tragic an event should mar your visit here. But what could we do? The panther was savage, a beast. To him our human laws could not apply. There was no other way— (SCHILL *appears fourth Bay Left with the gun. He looks dangerous. The* GIRLS *run off, screaming, Fourth Bay Right. The* TEACHER *follows the girls.*) Children—children—children!

CLAIRE. Anton, why are you frightening the children?

SCHILL. (*He works the bolt, loading the chamber, and raises the gun slowly.*) Go away, Claire— I warn you. Go away.

(*SOUND CUE #* 24.)

CLAIRE. How strange it is, Anton! How clearly it comes back to me! The day we saw one another for the first time, do you remember—I was on a balcony then. It was a day like today, a day in autumn without a breath of wind, warm as it is now—only lately I am always cold. You stood down there and stared at me without moving. I was embarrassed. I didn't know what to do. I wanted to go back into the darkness of the room where it was safe, but I couldn't. You stared up at me darkly, almost angrily, as if you wished to hurt me, but your eyes were full of passion. (SCHILL *begins to lower the gun, involuntarily.*) Then, I don't know why, I left the balcony and I came down and stood in the street beside you. You didn't greet me, you didn't say a word, but you took my hand and we walked together out of the town into the fields, and behind us came Kobby and Lobby, like two dogs, snivelling and giggling and snarling. Suddenly you picked up a stone and hurled it at them, and they ran yelping back into the town, and we were alone. (SCHILL *has lowered the rifle completely. He moves forward toward her as close as he can come.*) That was the beginning and everything else had to follow. There is no escape. (*She goes in and closes the shutters.* SCHILL *stands immobile. The* TEACHER *tiptoes in. He stares at* SCHILL, *who doesn't see him. Then he beckons to the children.*)

TEACHER. Come, children, sing. Sing.

(*They begin singing. He creeps behind* SCHILL *and snatches away the rifle.* SCHILL *turns sharply. The* PASTOR *comes in, Left.*)

PASTOR. Go, Schill—go!

(*The* CHILDREN *continue singing, moving across the Stage. The Golden Apostle vanishes.* [*SOUND CUE # 25.*] *The scene dissolves into the railway station setting, as in Act I* [*SOUND CUE # 25A.*] *But there are certain changes. The time-table marked* FAHRPLAN *is now new and the frame freshly painted. There is a new travel poster on the station wall. It has a yellow sun and the words,* REIST IN DEN SÜDEN. *On the other side of the Fahrplan is another poster with the words:* DIE PASSIONS-SPIELE OBERAMMERGAU. [*See Scene Design # 12.*] *The sound of passing* TRAINS *covers the scene-change.* [*SOUND CUE # 25B.*] SCHILL *appears with an old valise in his hand, dressed in a*

*shabby trench coat, his hat on his head. He looks
about with a furtive air, walking slowly to the platform. Slowly, as if by chance, the* TOWNSPEOPLE
enter, from all sides. SCHILL *hesitates, stops.*)

BURGOMASTER (*Enters Fifth Bay Right with* POLICE-
MAN.) Good evening, Schill.

SCHILL. Good evening.

POLICEMAN. Good evening. (*Comes Down Center with*
BURGOMASTER.)

SCHILL. Good evening. (*Crosses Left.*)

PAINTER. (*Enters First Bay Left.*) Good evening.

SCHILL. (*Crosses Right.*) Good evening.

DOCTOR. (*Enters First Bay Right*). Good evening.

SCHILL. (*Crosses Up Center.*) Good evening.

BURGOMASTER. So you're taking a little trip?

SCHILL. Yes. A little trip.

POLICEMAN. May one ask where to?

(*Other* TOWNSPEOPLE *enter from all directions during
this scene, giving the effect of surrounding* SCHILL.)

SCHILL. I don't know.

PAINTER. Don't know?

SCHILL. To Kalberstadt.

BURGOMASTER. (*With disbelief, pointing to the valise.*)
Kalberstadt?

SCHILL. After that—somewhere else.

PAINTER. Ah. After that somewhere else.

SCHILL. I thought maybe Australia.

BURGOMASTER. Australia!

ALL. Australia!

SCHILL. I'll raise the money somehow.

BURGOMASTER. But why Australia?

POLICEMAN. What would you be doing in Australia?

SCHILL. One can't always live in the same town, year
in year out.

PAINTER. But Australia—

DOCTOR. It's a risky trip for a man your age.

BURGOMASTER. One of the lady's little men ran off to Australia—

ALL. Yes.

POLICEMAN. You'll be much safer here.

PAINTER. Much!

SCHILL. (*He looks about him in anguish like a beast at bay. Low voice.*) I wrote a letter to the administration at Kaffigen.

BURGOMASTER. Yes?—And? (*They are* ALL *intent on the answer.*)

SCHILL. They didn't answer. (ALL *laugh.*)

DOCTOR. Do you mean to say you don't trust your old friends? That's not very flattering, you know.

BURGOMASTER. No one's going to do you any harm here.

DOCTOR. No harm here.

SCHILL. They didn't answer because the postmaster held up my letter.

PAINTER. Our postmaster? What an idea!

BURGOMASTER. The postmaster is a member of the town council.

POLICEMAN. A man of the utmost integrity.

DOCTOR. He doesn't hold up letters. What an idea!

(*The crossing bell starts ringing. The Local to Kalberstadt sounds in the distance.* [*SOUND CUE* # 26.])

STATION MASTER. (*Enters to edge of stage Down Left. Announces.*) Local to Kalberstadt!

(*The* TOWNSPEOPLE *all cross down to see the train arrive. Then they turn, with their backs to the audience, in a line across the stage.* SCHILL *cannot get through to reach the train.*)

SCHILL. (*In a low voice.*) What are you all doing here? What do you want of me?

BURGOMASTER. We don't like to see you go.

DOCTOR. We've come to see you off.

(*The sound of the approaching TRAIN grows louder.*)

SCHILL. I didn't ask you to come.
POLICEMAN. But we have come.
DOCTOR. As old friends.
ALL. As old friends.

(*The* STATION MASTER *holds up his paddle. The TRAIN stops with a screech of brakes. We hear the ENGINE panting Offstage.*)

BURGOMASTER. A pleasant journey.
DOCTOR. And long life!
PAINTER. And good luck in Australia! (*Crosses to* SCHILL *Up Center, and* OTHERS *follow as if to shake* SCHILL's *hand.*)
ALL. Yes, good luck in Australia.
SCHILL. (*Backing away.*) Why are you crowding me?
POLICEMAN. What's the matter now?

(*The* STATION MASTER *looks at his watch, then blows a long blast on his whistle.*)

SCHILL. Give me room.
DOCTOR. But you have plenty of room.

(*They* ALL *move away from him.*)

POLICEMAN. Better get aboard, Schill.
SCHILL. (*Pacing up and down nervously.*) I see. I see. One of you is going to push me under the wheels.
POLICEMAN. Oh, nonsense. Go on, get aboard.
SCHILL. Get away from me, all of you. (*Swings his valise and* ALL *back away.*)
BURGOMASTER. I don't know what you want. Just get on the train.
SCHILL. No. I know what you are going to do— I know what you are going to do.

DOCTOR. You're being ridiculous. Now, go on, get on the train.

SCHILL. Why are you all so near me?

DOCTOR. The man's gone mad.

STATION MASTER. 'Board! (*He blows his whistle. The engine bell clangs. The train starts to leave.*) [*SOUND CUE # 27.*]

BURGOMASTER. Get aboard, man. Quick.

(*The following speeches are spoken all together until the train noises fade away.*)

DOCTOR. The train's starting.

ALL. Get aboard, man. Get aboard. The train's starting.

SCHILL. If I try to get aboard, one of you will hold me back.

ALL. No, no.

BURGOMASTER. Get on the train.

SCHILL. (*In terror, crouches against the Right wall of the Station Master's office.*) No—no—no. No. (*Falling on his knees. The* OTHERS *crowd round him. He cowers on the ground abjectly. The TRAIN sounds fade away.*) Oh, no—no—don't push me, don't push me!

POLICEMAN. There. It's gone without you.

(*Slowly they leave him. He raises himself up to a sitting position, still trembling. A* TRUCK DRIVER *enters Third Right with an empty can.*)

TRUCK DRIVER. Do you know where I can get some water? My truck's boiling over. (SCHILL *points to the station office.*) Thanks. (*He enters the office, Left, gets the water and comes out. By this time,* SCHILL *is erect.* TRUCK DRIVER *crosses* SCHILL, *then stops and turns.*) Missed your train?

SCHILL. Yes.

TRUCK DRIVER. To Kalberstadt?

SCHILL. Yes.

TRUCK DRIVER. Well, come with me. I'm going that way.

SCHILL. This is my town. This is my home. (*With strange new dignity.*) No, thank you. I've changed my mind. I'm staying.

TRUCK DRIVER. (*He shrugs.*) All right. (*He goes out, Fourth Right.*)

(SCHILL *picks up his bag, looks Right and Left, and slowly walks off, Up Center between lampposts.*)

SLOW CURTAIN

ACT THREE

SCENE: *MUSIC is heard. Then the CURTAIN rises on the interior of the great barn, a dim cavernous structure. [See Scene Design # 13.] Bars of LIGHT fall across the shadowy forms, shafts of sunlight from the holes and cracks in the walls and roof. Overhead hangs an old ladder with rags and great cobwebs covering it. [SOUND CUE # 28.] Right, smoking a cigar, CLAIRE ZACHANASSIAN is sitting in her gilded sedan chair, motionless as an idol, in her magnificent bridal gown and veil. Near the chair stands an old cask.*

BOBBY. (*Comes in, Third Right, treading carefully.*) The Doctor and the teacher from the high school to see you, Madame.

CLAIRE. (*Impassive.*) Show them in.

(BOBBY *ushers them in, Third Right, as if they were entering a hall of state. The* TWO *grope their way through the litter. At last they find the lady and bow. They are both well dressed in new clothes, but very dusty.*)

BOBBY. Doctor Nüsslin and Professor Müller. (*He exits Third Right.*)

DOCTOR. Madame.

CLAIRE. You look dusty, gentlemen.

DOCTOR. (*Dusts himself off vigorously.*) Oh, forgive us. We had to climb over an old carriage.

TEACHER. Our respects.

DOCTOR. A fabulous wedding.

TEACHER. Beautiful occasion.

CLAIRE. It's stifling here. But I love this old barn. The smell of hay and old straw and axle-grease—it is the scent of my youth. Sit down. (DOCTOR *sits on straw*

65

basket.) All this rubbish—the haycart, the old carriage, the cask, even the pitchfork—it was all here when I was a girl.

TEACHER. (*Gets barrel and comes Downstage.*) Remarkable place. (*He mops his brow.*)

CLAIRE. I thought the pastor's text was very appropriate. The lesson a trifle long.

TEACHER. 1 Corinthians 13.

CLAIRE. Your choristers sang beautifully, Professor.

TEACHER. Bach. From the Saint Matthew Passion.

DOCTOR. Güllen has never seen such magnificence! The flowers! The jewels! And the people.

TEACHER. (*He sits on barrel.*) The theatrical world, the world of finance, the world of art, the world of science—

CLAIRE. All these worlds are now back in their Cadillacs speeding toward the capital for the wedding reception. But I'm sure you didn't come here to talk about them.

DOCTOR. Dear lady, we should not intrude on your valuable time. Your husband must be waiting impatiently.

CLAIRE. No, no, I've packed him off to Brazil.

DOCTOR. To Brazil, Madame?

CLAIRE. Yes. For his honeymoon.

TEACHER *and* DOCTOR. Oh! But your wedding guests?

CLAIRE. I've planned a delightful dinner for them. They'll never miss me. Now what was it you wished to talk about?

TEACHER. About— (*Hesitates.*)

CLAIRE. Yes, well, what?

TEACHER. Anton Schill, Madame.

CLAIRE. Is he dead?

TEACHER. (*Rises.*) Madame, we may be poor. But we have our principles.

CLAIRE. I see. Then what do you want?

TEACHER. (*He mops his brow again, moves a step toward* CLAIRE.) The fact is, Madame, in anticipation of your well-known munificence, that is, feeling that you would give the town some sort of gift, we have all been buying things. Necessities—

DOCTOR. With money we don't have.

(*The* TEACHER *blows his nose.*)

CLAIRE. You've run into debt?

DOCTOR. Up to here.

CLAIRE. In spite of your principles?

TEACHER. We're human, Madame.

CLAIRE. I see.

TEACHER. We have been poor a long time. A long, long time.

DOCTOR. (*He rises.*) The question is, how are we going to pay?

CLAIRE. You already know.

TEACHER. (*Courageously.*) I beg you, Madame Zachanassian, put yourself in our position for a moment. For twenty-two years I've been cudgeling my brains to plant a few seeds of knowledge in this wilderness. And all this time, my gallant colleague, Doctor Nüsslin, has been rattling around in his ancient Mercedes from patient to patient trying to keep these wretches alive. Why? Why have we spent our lives in this miserable hole? For money? Hardly. The pay is ridiculous.

DOCTOR. And yet, the Professor here has declined an offer to head the high school in Kalberstadt.

TEACHER. And Doctor Nüsslin has refused an important post at the University of Erlangen. Madame, the simple fact is, we love our town. We were born here. It is our life.

DOCTOR. That's true.

TEACHER. What has kept us going all these years is the hope that one day the community will prosper again as it did in the days when we were young.

CLAIRE. Good.

TEACHER. Madame, there is no reason for our poverty. We suffer here from a mysterious blight. We have factories. They stand idle. There is oil in the valley of Pückenried.

DOCTOR. There is copper under the Konradsweil forest. There is power in our streams, in our waterfalls.

TEACHER. We are not poor, Madame. If we had credit, if we had confidence, the factories would open, orders and commissions would pour in. And our economy would bloom together with our cultural life. We would become once again like the towns around us, healthy and prosperous.

DOCTOR. If the Wagonworks were put on its feet again—

TEACHER. The Foundry.

DOCTOR. The Golden Eagle Pencil Factory.

TEACHER. Buy these plants, Madame. Put them in operation once more, and I swear to you, Güllen will flourish and it will bless you. We don't need a billion marks. Ten million, properly invested, would give us back our life, and incidentally return to the investor an excellent dividend. Save us, Madame. Save us, and we will not only bless you, we will make money for you.

CLAIRE. I don't need money.

DOCTOR. (*Crosses to Down Right of her chair.*) Madame, we are not asking for charity. This is business.

CLAIRE. It's a good idea . . .

DOCTOR. Dear lady! I knew you wouldn't let us down.

CLAIRE. But it's out of the question. I cannot buy the Wagonworks. I already own them.

DOCTOR. The Wagonworks?

TEACHER. And the Foundry?

CLAIRE. And the Foundry.

DOCTOR. And the Golden Eagle pencil factory?

CLAIRE. Everything. The valley of Pückenried with its oil, the forest of Konradsweil with its ore, the barn, the town, the streets, the houses, the shops, everything. I had my agents buy up this rubbish over the years, bit by bit, piece by piece, until I had it all. Your hopes were an illusion, your vision empty, your self-sacrifice a stupidity, your whole life completely senseless.

TEACHER. Then the mysterious blight—

CLAIRE. The mysterious blight was I.

DOCTOR. But this is monstrous! (*Crosses Down Left to basket.* TEACHER *turns Upstage.*)

CLAIRE. Monstrous. I was seventeen when I left this town. It was winter. I was dressed in a cotton sailor suit and my red braids hung down my back. I was in my seventh month. As I walked down the street to the station, the boys whistled after me, and threw stones. I sat freezing in my seat in the Hamburg Express. But before the roof of the great barn was lost behind the trees, I had made up my mind that one day I would come back.

TEACHER. (*Turns to face her.*) But Madame—

CLAIRE. (*She smiles.*) And now I have. (*She claps her hands.*) Mike. Max. Take me back to The Golden Apostle. I've been here long enough.

(MIKE *and* MAX *enter Third Right and start to pick up the sedan chair.* TEACHER *pushes* MIKE *away.*)

TEACHER. Madame. One moment. Please. I see it all now. I had thought of you as an avenging fury, a Medea, a Clytemnestra—but I was wrong. You are a warm-hearted woman who has suffered a terrible injustice and now you have returned and taught us an unforgettable lesson. You have stripped us bare. But now that we stand before you naked, I know you will set aside these thoughts of vengeance. If we made you suffer, you too have put us through the fire. Have mercy, Madame.

CLAIRE. When I have had justice. Mike! (*She signals to* MIKE *and* MAX *to pick up the sedan chair. They cross the stage. The* TEACHER *bars the way.*)

TEACHER. But, Madame, one injustice cannot cure another. What good will it do to force us into crime? Horror succeeds horror, shame is piled on shame. It settles nothing.

CLAIRE. It settles everything. (*They move Upstage toward the exit, Right, 5. The* TEACHER *follows.*)

TEACHER. Madame, this lesson you have taught us will never be forgotten. We will hand it down from father to son. It will be a monument more lasting than any vengeance. Whatever we have been, in the future we shall be better because of you. You have pushed us to the extreme. Now forgive us. Show us the way to a better life. Have pity, Madame—pity. (*He kneels in front of the chair and it stops.*) That is the highest justice.

CLAIRE. The highest justice has no pity. It is bright and pure and clear. The world made me into a whore; now I make the world into a brothel. Those who wish to go down, may go down. Those who wish to dance with me, may dance with me. (*To her* PORTERS.) Go.

(*She is carried off, Fifth Right. The LIGHTS black out. [SOUND CUE # 29.] Down Right, appears* SCHILL's *shop. It has a new sign, a new counter. [See Scene Design # 14.] The door bell, when it rings, has an impressive sound.* FRAU SCHILL *stands behind the counter in a new dress. All* TOWNSPEOPLE *are on stage at opening to strike and bring on props. Then they exit, laughing in all directions.* FIRST MAN *remains behind. He is dressed as a prosperous butcher, a few bloodstains on his snowy apron, a gold watch chain across his open vest.*)

FIRST MAN. What a wedding! I'll swear the whole town was there. Cigarettes.

FRAU SCHILL. Clara is entitled to a little happiness after all. I'm happy for her. Green or white?

FIRST MAN. Turkish. The bridesmaids! Dancers and opera singers. And the dresses! Down to here.

FRAU SCHILL. It's the fashion nowadays.

FIRST MAN. Reporters! Photographers! From all over the world! (*In a low voice.*) They will be here any minute.

FRAU SCHILL. (*Downstage of counter.*) What have reporters to do with us? We are simple people, Herr Hofbauer. There is nothing for them here.

FIRST MAN. (*Moves away from her.*) They're questioning everybody. They're asking everything. (*Lights a cigarette. He looks up at the ceiling.*) Footsteps.

FRAU SCHILL. (*Crosses behind counter.*) He's pacing the room. Up and down. Day and night.

FIRST MAN. Haven't seen him all week.

FRAU SCHILL. He never goes out.

FIRST MAN. (*Crosses and sits counter.*) It's his conscience. That was pretty mean, the way he treated poor Madame Zachanassian.

FRAU SCHILL. (*Moves to Right of him.*) That's true. I feel very badly about it myself.

FIRST MAN. To ruin a young girl like that— God doesn't forgive it. (FRAU SCHILL *nods solemnly with pursed lips. The* BUTCHER *gives her a level glance.*) Look, I hope he'll have sense enough to keep his mouth shut in front of the reporters.

FRAU SCHILL. I certainly hope so.

FIRST MAN. You know his character.

FRAU SCHILL. Only too well, Herr Hofbauer.

FIRST MAN. If he tries to throw dirt at our Clara and tell a lot of lies, how she tried to get us to kill him, which anyway she never meant—

FRAU SCHILL. Of course not.

FIRST MAN. —then we'll really have to do something! And not because of the money— (*He spits.*) But out of ordinary human decency. God knows Madame Zachanassian has suffered enough through him already.

FRAU SCHILL. She has indeed.

TEACHER. (*He comes in Fourth Right. He is not quite sober. Crosses to Center and looks about the shop.*) Has the press been here yet?

FIRST MAN. No.

TEACHER. It's not my custom, as you know, Frau Schill—but I wonder if I could have a strong alcoholic drink?

FRAU SCHILL. (*Crosses behind counter, gets bottle and glass.*) It's an honor to serve you, Herr Professor. I have a good Steinhäger. Would you like to try a glass?

TEACHER. (*Crossing to counter.*) A very small glass.

FRAU SCHILL. (*She serves bottle and glass. The* TEACHER *tosses off a glass.*) Your hand is shaking, Herr Professor.

TEACHER. To tell the truth, I have been drinking a little already.

FRAU SCHILL. Have another glass. It will do you good.

TEACHER. (*He accepts another glass. Takes bottle, crosses to bench, sits.*) Is that him up there, walking?

FRAU SCHILL. Up and down. Up and down.

FIRST MAN. It's God punishing him.

(*The* PAINTER *comes in with* KARL *and* OTTILIE, *Fourth Right.*)

PAINTER. Careful! A reporter just asked us the way to this shop.

FIRST MAN. I hope you didn't tell him.

PAINTER. I told him we were strangers here.

(*They* ALL *laugh. The door opens. The* SECOND MAN *darts into the shop.*)

SECOND MAN. Look out, everybody! The press! They are across the street in your shop, Hofbauer.

FIRST MAN. My boy will know how to deal with them.

SECOND MAN. Make sure Schill doesn't come down, Hofbauer.

FIRST MAN. Leave that to me.

(*They group themselves about the shop.*)

TEACHER. Listen to me, all of you. When the reporters come I'm going to speak to them. I'm going to make a statement. A statement to the world in behalf of myself as Rector of Güllen High School and in behalf of you all, for all your sakes. (*He rises and moves Left of bench.*)

PAINTER. What are you going to say?

TEACHER. I shall tell the truth about Claire Zachanassian.

FRAU SCHILL. (*Crosses and snatches bottle from him.*) You're drunk, Herr Professor, you should be ashamed of yourself. (*Returns behind counter.*)

TEACHER. I should be ashamed? You should all be ashamed!

SON. Shut your trap. You're drunk.

DAUGHTER. Please, Professor—

TEACHER. (*Crosses to Upstage end of counter.*) Girl, you disappoint me. It is your place to speak. But you are silent and you force your old teacher to raise his voice. I am going to speak the truth. It is my duty and I am not afraid. The world may not wish to listen, but no one can silence me. (*Crosses toward door Up Right.*) I'm not going to wait—I'm going over to Hofbauer's shop now.

ALL. No, you're not. Stop him. Stop him.

(*They* ALL *spring at the* TEACHER. *He defends himself. At this moment,* SCHILL *appears, through Fourth Left. In contrast to the others, he is dressed shabbily in an old black jacket, his best.*)

SCHILL. (*Crosses to Center.*) What's going on in my shop? (*The* TOWNSMEN *let go the* TEACHER *and turn to stare at* SCHILL.) What's the trouble, Professor?

TEACHER. (*Crosses to* SCHILL.) Schill, I am speaking out at last! I am going to tell the press everything.

SCHILL. Be quiet, Professor.

TEACHER. What did you say?

SCHILL. Be quiet. (*Turns away.*)

TEACHER. You want me to be quiet?

SCHILL. Please.

TEACHER. But, Schill, if I keep quiet, if you miss this opportunity—they're over in Hofbauer's shop now . . .

SCHILL. Please. (*Crosses Down Left Center.*)

TEACHER. As you wish. If you too are on their side, I have no more to say. (*Sits on bench.*)

(*The DOORBELL jingles. A* REPORTER *comes in, Fourth Right.*)

REPORTER. (*Crossing to Center.*) Is Anton Schill here? (*Moves to* SCHILL.) Are you Herr Schill?

SCHILL. What?

REPORTER. Herr Schill.

SCHILL. (*Moves behind counter.*) Er—no. Herr Schill's gone to Kalberstadt for the day.

REPORTER. Oh, thank you. Good day. (*He goes out, Fourth Right.*)

PAINTER. (*Mops his brow.*) Whew! Close shave. (*He follows the* REPORTER *out.*)

SECOND MAN. (*Walking up to* SCHILL.) That was pretty smart of you to keep your mouth shut. You know what to expect if you don't. (*He goes, Fourth Right.*)

FIRST MAN. (*Crosses to counter.*) Give me a Havana. (SCHILL *serves him.*) You bastard! (*He goes Fourth Right.* SCHILL *opens his account book.*)

FRAU SCHILL. Come along, children— (FRAU SCHILL, *the* SON *and the* DAUGHTER *go off, Fourth Left.*)

TEACHER. They're going to kill you. I've known it all along, and you too, you must have known it. The need is too strong, the temptation too great. And now perhaps I too will join against you. (*Crosses to him.*) I belong to them and, like them, I can feel myself hardening into something that is not human—not beautiful.

SCHILL. It can't be helped.

TEACHER. Pull yourself together, man. Speak to the reporters, you've no time to lose.

SCHILL. (*He looks up from his account book.*) No. I'm not going to fight any more.

TEACHER. Are you so frightened that you don't dare open your mouth?

SCHILL. I made Claire what she is. I made myself what I am. What should I do? Should I pretend that I'm innocent?

TEACHER. No, you can't. You are as guilty as hell.

SCHILL. Yes.

TEACHER. You are a bastard.

SCHILL. Yes.

TEACHER. But that does not justify your murder. (SCHILL *looks at him.*) I wish I could believe that for what they're doing—for what they're going to do—they will suffer for the rest of their lives. But it's not true. In a little while they will have justified everything and forgotten everything.

SCHILL. Of course.

TEACHER. Your name will never again be mentioned in this town. That's how it will be.

SCHILL. I don't hold it against you.

TEACHER. But I do. I will hold it against myself all my life. Give me a bottle of schnapps. (SCHILL *does.*) And charge it.

(*The DOORBELL jingles. The* BURGOMASTER *comes in Fourth Right. The* TEACHER *stares at him, then goes out without another word, Fourth Right, hiding bottle under his jacket.*)

BURGOMASTER. (*Crosses Center.*) Good afternoon, Schill. Don't let me disturb you. I've just dropped in for a moment.

SCHILL. I'm just finishing my accounts for the week.

(*A moment's pause.*)

BURGOMASTER. The town council meets tonight. At The Golden Apostle. In the auditorium.

SCHILL. I'll be there.

BURGOMASTER. The whole town will be there. Your case will be discussed and final action taken. You've put us in a pretty tight spot, you know.

SCHILL. Yes. I'm sorry.

BURGOMASTER. The lady's offer will be rejected.

SCHILL. Possibly.

BURGOMASTER. Of course, I may be wrong.

SCHILL. Of course.

BURGOMASTER. In that case—are you prepared to accept the judgment of the town? The meeting will be covered by the press, you know.

SCHILL. By the press?

BURGOMASTER. Yes, and the radio and the newsreel. It's a very ticklish situation. Not only for you—believe me, it's even worse for us. What with the wedding, and all the publicity, we've become famous. All of a sudden our ancient democratic institutions have become of interest to the world.

SCHILL. Are you going to make the condition public?

BURGOMASTER. No, no, of course not. Not directly. We will have to put the matter to a vote—that is unavoidable. But only those involved will understand.

SCHILL. I see.

BURGOMASTER. As far as the press is concerned, you are simply the intermediary between us and Madame Zachanassian. I have whitewashed you completely.

SCHILL. That is very generous of you.

BURGOMASTER. (*Moves in to counter.*) Frankly, it's not for your sake, but for the sake of your family. They have been honest and decent.

SCHILL. Oh—

BURGOMASTER. So far we've all played fair. You've kept your mouth shut and so have we. (*Leans on counter.*) Now can we continue to depend on you? Because if you have any idea of opening your mouth at tonight's meeting, there won't be any meeting.

SCHILL. I'm glad to hear an open threat at last.

BURGOMASTER. We are not threatening you. You are threatening us. If you speak, you force us to act—in advance.

SCHILL. That won't be necessary.

BURGOMASTER. So if the town decides against you?

SCHILL. I will accept their decision.

BURGOMASTER. Good. (*A moment's pause.*) I'm delighted to see there is still a spark of decency left in you. But—wouldn't it be better if we didn't have to call a meeting at all? (*He pauses. He takes a gun from his pocket, puts it on the counter.*) I've brought you this.

SCHILL. Thank you.

BURGOMASTER. It's loaded.

SCHILL. I don't need a gun.

BURGOMASTER. (*He clears his throat.*) You see? We could tell the lady that we had condemned you in secret session and you had anticipated our decision. (*Moves away to Center.*) I've lost a lot of sleep getting to this point, believe me.

SCHILL. I believe you.

BURGOMASTER. (*Turns to him.*) Frankly, in your place, I myself would prefer to take the path of honor. Get it over with, once and for all. Don't you agree? For the sake of your friends! For the sake of our children, your own children—you have a daughter, a son— Schill, you know our need, our misery.

SCHILL. You've put me through hell, you and your town. You were my friend, you smiled and reassured me. But day by day I saw you change—your shoes, your ties, your suits—your hearts. If you had been honest with me then, perhaps I would feel differently toward you now. I might even use that gun you brought me. For the sake of my friends. But now I have conquered my fear. Alone. It was hard, but it's done. And now you will have to judge me. I will accept your judgment. For me that will be justice. How it will be for you, I don't know. (*He turns away.*) You may kill me if you like. I won't complain, I won't protest, I won't defend myself. But I won't do your job for you either.

BURGOMASTER. (*Takes up his gun, puts it into his pocket.*) There it is. You've had your chance and you won't take it. Too bad. (*He takes out a cigarette.*) I suppose it's more than we can expect of a man like you. (SCHILL *lights the* BURGOMASTER'S *cigarette.*) Good day.

SCHILL. Good day. (*He goes.* FRAU SCHILL, SON *and* DAUGHTER *come in, fourth Right.* FRAU SCHILL *is dressed in a fur coat. The* DAUGHTER *is in a new red dress. The* SON *has a new sports jacket.*) What a beautiful coat, Mathilde!

FRAU SCHILL. Real fur. You like it?

SCHILL. Should I? What a lovely dress, Ottilie!

DAUGHTER. (*Spins around.*) C'est très chic, n'est-ce-pas?

SCHILL. What?

FRAU SCHILL. Ottilie is taking a course in French.

SCHILL. Very useful. (*Crosses to fourth Left.*) Karl—whose automobile is that out there at the curb?

SON. Oh, it's only an Opel. They're not expensive.

SCHILL. (*Crosses to Center.*) You bought yourself a car?

SON. On credit. Easiest thing in the world.

FRAU SCHILL. (*Moves Right of* SCHILL.) Everyone's buying on credit now, Anton. These fears of yours are ridiculous. You'll see. Clara has a good heart. She only means to teach you a lesson. (*Church BELLS start ringing.*) [*SOUND CUE # 30.*]

DAUGHTER. (*Moves to* SCHILL.) She means to teach you a lesson, that's all.

SON. It's high time you got the point, Father.

SCHILL. I get the point. Listen. The bells of Güllen. Do you hear?

SON. Yes, we have four bells now. It sounds quite good.

DAUGHTER. Just as in Gray's *Elegy.*

SCHILL. What?

FRAU SCHILL. Ottilie is taking a course in English literature.

SCHILL. Congratulations. (*Crosses to* SON.) It's Sunday. I should very much like to take a ride in your car. Our car.

SON. You want to ride in the car?

SCHILL. Why not? I want to ride through the Konradsweil Forest. I want to see the town where I've lived all my life.

FRAU SCHILL. I don't think that will look very nice for any of us.

SCHILL. No—perhaps not. Well, I'll walk.

FRAU SCHILL. Then take us to Kalberstadt, Karl, and we'll go to a cinema.

SCHILL. A cinema? It's a good idea.

FRAU SCHILL. (*She moves Up Left Center with* SON *and* DAUGHTER.) See you soon, Anton.

SCHILL. Good-bye, Ottilie. Good-bye, Karl. Good-bye, Mathilde.

FAMILY. Good-bye. (*They go out, Fourth Left.*)

SCHILL. Good-bye.

(*The shop sign is flown.* [*SOUND CUE* # 31.] *The LIGHTS black out. They come up at once on the forest scene.* [*See Scene Design* # 15.] SCHILL *walks a few steps, looking at the trees.*)

SCHILL. Even the forest has turned to gold. (*He sits on the bench.* CLAIRE'S *voice is heard Offstage.*)

CLAIRE. (*Offstage.*) Stop. Wait here. (CLAIRE *comes in Fifth Right. She gazes slowly up at the trees, picks at some leaves. Then she walks slowly Down Center. She stops before a tree, glances up the trunk.*) Bark-borers. The old tree is dying. (*She catches sight of* SCHILL.)

SCHILL. Clara. (*He rises.*)

CLAIRE. How pleasant to see you here. I was visiting my forest. May I sit by you?

SCHILL. Oh, yes. Please do. (*They sit together.*) I've just been saying good-bye to my family. They've gone to the cinema. Karl has bought himself a car.

CLAIRE. How nice.

SCHILL. Ottilie is taking French lessons. And a course in English literature.

CLAIRE. You see? They're beginning to take an interest in higher things.

SCHILL. Listen. A finch. You hear?

CLAIRE. Yes. It's a finch. And a cuckoo in the distance. Would you like some music?

SCHILL. Oh, yes. That would be very nice.

CLAIRE. Anything special?

SCHILL. "Deep in the Forest."

CLAIRE. Your favorite song. They know it. (*She raises her hand. The mandolin and guitar play the tune softly.*) [*SOUND CUE* # 31.]

SCHILL. We had a child?

CLAIRE. Yes.

SCHILL. Boy or girl?

CLAIRE. Girl.

SCHILL. What name did you give her?

CLAIRE. I called her Genevieve.

SCHILL. That's a very pretty name.

CLAIRE. Yes.

SCHILL. What was she like?

CLAIRE. I saw her only once. When she was born. Then they took her away from me.

SCHILL. Her eyes?

CLAIRE. They weren't open yet.

SCHILL. Her hair?

CLAIRE. Black, I think. It's usually black at first.

SCHILL. Yes, of course. Where did she die, Clara?

CLAIRE. In some family. I've forgotten their name. Meningitis, they said. The officials wrote me a letter.

SCHILL. Oh, I'm so very sorry, Clara.

CLAIRE. I've told you about our child. Now tell me about myself.

SCHILL. About yourself?

CLAIRE. Yes. How I was when I was seventeen in the days when you loved me.

SCHILL. I remember one day you waited for me in the great barn. I had to look all over the place for you. At last I found you lying in the haycart with nothing on and a long straw between your lips . . .

CLAIRE. Yes. I was pretty in those days.

SCHILL. You were beautiful.

CLAIRE. You were strong. The time you fought those two railway men who were following me, I wiped the blood from your face with my red petticoat. (*The MUSIC ends.*) They've stopped.

SCHILL. Tell them to play "Thoughts of Home."

CLAIRE. They know that too. (*She raises hand and the MUSIC plays.*) [*SOUND CUE # 33.*]

SCHILL. Here we are, Clara, sitting together in our forest for the last time. The town council meets tonight. They will condemn me to death and one of them will kill me. I don't know who and I don't know where. Clara, I only know that in a little while a useless life will come to an end. (*He bows his head on her bosom. She takes him in her arms, tenderly.*)

CLAIRE. I shall take you in your coffin to Capri. You will have your tomb in the park of my villa, where I can see you from my bedroom window. White marble and onyx in a grove of green cypress. With a beautiful view of the Mediterranean.

SCHILL. I've always wanted to see it.

CLAIRE. Your love for me died years ago, Anton. But my love for you would not die. It turned into something strong like the hidden roots of the forest, something evil like white mushrooms that grow unseen in the darkness. And slowly it reached out for your life. Now I have you. You are mine. Alone. At last, and forever, a peaceful ghost in a silent house. (*The MUSIC ends.*)

SCHILL. The song is over.

CLAIRE. Adieu, Anton. (CLAIRE *kisses* ANTON, *a long kiss. Then she rises and moves towards exit, Second Right.*)

SCHILL. Adieu.

(SCHILL *remains sitting on the bench. A row of lamps descends from the flies.* [*SOUND CUE # 34.*] *The* TOWNSPEOPLE *come in from both sides, each bearing his chair. A table and chairs are set Up Center.* [*See Scene Design # 16.*] *On both sides sit the* TOWNSPEOPLE, *all in new Sunday clothes. The* POLICEMAN, *in a new uniform sits on the bench behind* SCHILL. *Around them are* TECHNICIANS *of all sorts with lights, cameras and other equipment. The* TOWNSWOMEN *are absent. They do not vote. The* BURGOMASTER *takes his place at the table,*

Center. The DOCTOR *and the* PASTOR *sit at the same table, at his Right, and the* TEACHER *in his academic gown, at his Left.*)

BURGOMASTER. (*At a sign from the* RADIO TECHNICIAN, *he pounds the floor with his wand of office.*) Fellow citizens of Güllen, I call this meeting to order. The agenda: there is only one matter before us. I have the honor to announce officially that Madame Claire Zachanassian, daughter of our beloved citizen, the famous architect Siegfried Wäscher, has decided to make a gift to the town of one billion marks. Five hundred million to the town, five hundred million to be divided per capita among the citizens. After certain necessary preliminaries, a vote will be taken, and you, as citizens of Güllen, will signify your will by a show of hands. Has anyone any objection to this mode of procedure? The Pastor? (*Silence.*) The Police? (*Silence.*) The Town Health Official? (*Silence.*) The Rector of Güllen High School? (*Silence.*) The political opposition? (*Silence.*) I shall then proceed to the vote— (*The* TEACHER *rises. The* BURGOMASTER *turns in surprise and irritation.*) You wish to speak?

TEACHER. Yes.

BURGOMASTER. Very well. (*He moves to Left of table,* TEACHER *to Center. The movie camera starts running.*)

TEACHER. Fellow townsmen. (*The* PHOTOGRAPHER *flashes a bulb in his face.*) Fellow townsmen. We all know that by means of this gift, Madame Claire Zachanassian intends to attain a certain object. What is this object? To enrich the town of her youth, yes. (BURGOMASTER *sits.*) But more than that, she desires by means of this gift to re-establish justice among us. This desire expressed by our benefactress raises an all-important question. Is it true that our community harbors in its soul such a burden of guilt?

BURGOMASTER. Yes! True!

SECOND MAN. Crimes are concealed among us.

THIRD MAN. (*He jumps up.*) Sins!

FOURTH MAN. (*He jumps up also.*) Perjuries.

PAINTER. Justice!

CRIES. Justice! Justice!

TEACHER. Citizens of Güllen, this then is the simple fact of the case. We have participated in an injustice. I thoroughly recognize the material advantages which this gift opens to us. I do not overlook the fact that it is poverty which is the root of all this bitterness and evil. Nevertheless, there is no question here of money.

CRIES. No! No!

TEACHER. Here there is no question of our prosperity as a community or our well-being as individuals—the question is—must be—whether or not we wish to live according to the principles of justice, those principles for which our forefathers lived and fought and for which they died, those principles which form the soul of our Western culture.

TOWNSPEOPLE. Hear! Hear! (*Applause.*)

TEACHER. (*Desperately, realizing that he is fighting a losing battle, and on the verge of hysteria. Moves to front of table.*) Wealth has meaning only when benevolence comes of it, but only he who hungers for grace will receive grace. Do you feel this hunger, my fellow citizens, this hunger of the spirit, or do you feel only that other profane hunger, the hunger of the body? That is the question which I, as Rector of your high school, now propound to you. Only if you can no longer tolerate the presence of evil among you, only if you can in no circumstances endure a world in which injustice exists, are you worthy to receive Madame Zachanassian's billion. If not— (*Wild applause. He gestures desperately for silence.* PHOTOGRAPHER *takes a flash.*) If not, then God have mercy on us!

(*The* TOWNSPEOPLE *crowd around him, ambiguously, somewhere between threat and congratulation. He takes his seat, utterly crushed, exhausted by his effort. The* BURGOMASTER *advances and takes charge once again. Order is restored.*)

BURGOMASTER. Anton Schill— (*The* POLICEMAN *gives* SCHILL *a shove.* SCHILL *gets up.*) Anton Schill, it is through you that this gift is offered to the town. Are you willing that this offer should be accepted?

(SCHILL *mumbles something.* PHOTOGRAPHER *runs to Center and takes flash.*)

RADIO REPORTER. You'll have to speak up a little, Herr Schill.

SCHILL. Yes.

BURGOMASTER. Will you respect our decision in the matter before us?

SCHILL. I will respect your decision.

BURGOMASTER. (*Moves Center.*) Then I proceed to the vote. All those who are in accord with the terms on which this gift is offered will signify the same by raising their right hands. (*After a moment, the* POLICEMAN *raises his hand. Then one by one the* OTHERS. *Last of all, the* TEACHER. SCHILL *does not vote.*) All against? The offer is accepted. (SCHILL *sits.*) I now solemnly call upon you, fellow townsmen, to declare in the face of all the world that you take this action not out of love for worldly gain—

TOWNSMEN. (*Raise their hands. In chorus:*) Not out of love for worldly gain—

BURGOMASTER. But out of love for the right.

TOWNSMEN. But out of love for the right.

BURGOMASTER. We join together, now, as brothers—

TOWNSMEN. We join together, now, as brothers—

BURGOMASTER. To purify our town of guilt—

TOWNSMEN. To purify our town of guilt—

BURGOMASTER. And to reaffirm our faith—

TOWNSMEN. And to reaffirm our faith—

BURGOMASTER. In the eternal power of justice.

TOWNSMEN. In the eternal power of justice.

(*The LIGHTS go off suddenly.*)

SCHILL. (*Jumps up. A scream.*) Oh, God!

THE CAMERA MAN. I'm sorry, Herr Burgomaster. We seem to have blown a fuse. (*The LIGHTS go on.*) Ah— there we are. Would you mind doing that last bit again?

BURGOMASTER. (*Steps forward.*) Again?

THE CAMERA MAN. (*Walks forward.*) Yes, for the newsreel.

BURGOMASTER. Oh, the newsreel. Certainly.

THE CAMERA MAN. Ready now? Right.

BURGOMASTER. And to reaffirm our faith—

TOWNSMEN. And to reaffirm our faith—

BURGOMASTER. In the eternal power of justice.

TOWNSMEN. In the eternal power of justice.

THE CAMERA MAN. (*To his* ASSISTANT.) Too bad he didn't scream "Oh God" again. (*The* ASSISTANT *shrugs.*)

BURGOMASTER. Fellow citizens of Güllen, I declare this meeting adjourned. The ladies and gentlemen of the press will find refreshments served downstairs with the compliments of the town council. The exits lead directly to the restaurant.

THE CAMERA MAN. Thank you.

(*The* NEWSMEN *go off with alacrity, Left and Right, carrying off their chairs. The* TOWNSMEN *remain on the Stage.* SCHILL *gets up.*)

POLICEMAN. (*Pushes* SCHILL *down.*) Sit down.

SCHILL. Is it to be now?

POLICEMAN. Naturally, now.

SCHILL. I thought it would be so much better to have it at my house.

POLICEMAN. It will be here.

BURGOMASTER. Lower the lights. (*The LIGHTS dim as* SECOND *and* THIRD MEN *get poles Right and raise them to lamps.*) Are they all gone?

VOICE. (*Off.*) All gone.

BURGOMASTER. The gallery?

SECOND VOICE. (*Off.*) Empty.

BURGOMASTER. Lock the doors.

THE VOICE. (*Off.*) Locked here.

SECOND VOICE. (*Off.*) Locked here.

BURGOMASTER. Form a lane. (*The* MEN *form a lane. At the end stands the* ATHLETE *in elegant white slacks, a red scarf around his singlet.*) Pastor. Will you be so good?

PASTOR. (*He walks slowly to* SCHILL.) Anton Schill, your heavy hour has come.

SCHILL. May I have a cigarette?

PASTOR. Cigarette, Burgomaster.

BURGOMASTER. (*Crosses to* SCHILL.) Of course. With pleasure. And a good one. (*He offers his case to* SCHILL *who takes one. The* POLICEMAN *lights the cigarette.*)

PASTOR. In the words of the prophet Amos—

SCHILL. Please— (*He shakes his head.*)

PASTOR. You're no longer afraid?

SCHILL. No. I'm not afraid.

PASTOR. I will pray for you.

SCHILL. Pray for us all. (*The* PASTOR *bows his head.*)

BURGOMASTER. Anton Schill, stand up! (SCHILL *hesitates.*)

POLICEMAN. Stand up, you swine!

BURGOMASTER. Schultz, please.

POLICEMAN. I'm sorry. I was carried away.

(SCHILL *walks slowly to Center and turns his back on the audience, then gives cigarette to the* POLICEMAN, *who steps on it.*)

BURGOMASTER. Enter the lane.

(SCHILL *hesitates a moment. He goes slowly into the lane of silent* MEN. *The* ATHLETE *stares at him from the opposite end.* SCHILL *looks in turn at the hard faces of those who surround him, and sinks slowly to his knees. The lane contracts silently into a knot as the* MEN *close in and crouch over. They drag* SCHILL *Downstage. Complete silence. The knot of* MEN *pulls back slowly. Then it opens. Only the*

DOCTOR *is left, kneeling by the corpse. The* DOCTOR *rises and takes off his stethoscope.*)

PASTOR. Is it all over?
DOCTOR. Heart failure.
BURGOMASTER. Died of joy.
ALL. Died of joy.

(ALL *move away, forming groups of two and three on either side of Stage, and* ALL *light cigarettes. A cloud of smoke rises above them. At same time, the* TEACHER *moves to Right of* SCHILL *and covers him with his gown; then the* TEACHER *crosses to* POLICEMAN, *who hands him a lighted cigarette, From Fifth Right comes* CLAIRE ZACHANASSIAN, *dressed in black, followed by* BOBBY. *She walks slowly to Center and looks down at the body of* SCHILL.)

CLAIRE. Uncover him. (BOBBY *uncovers* SCHILL'S *face. She stares at it a long moment. She sighs.*) Cover his face.

(BOBBY *covers it.* CLAIRE *goes out, Fifth Right.* BOBBY *takes the check from his wallet, holds it out to the* BURGOMASTER, *who, after a moment's hesitation, walks over from the knot of silent* MEN. *He holds out his hand for the check. The LIGHTS fade.*)
[*SOUND CUE* # 35.]

(*At once the sound of an approaching train is heard, and the scene dissolves into the setting of the Railway Station. The gradual transformation of the shabby town into a thing of elegance and beauty is now accomplished. The Railway Station glitters with neon LIGHTS and is surrounded with garlands, bright posters, and flags. What is seen of the town indicates the culmination of the change from squalor to a blinding and somewhat technical perfection.* [*See Scene Design* # 17.] *The* TOWNSFOLK, *men and women, now in brand new clothes, form them-*

selves into a group in front of the station. The
sound of the approaching TRAIN grows louder.
The TRAIN stops and LIGHTS come up full. The
church BELLS start pealing. [SOUND CUE #
35A.] Now come the TWO BLIND MEN, then BOBBY,
MIKE and MAX carrying the coffin shoulder high,
lastly CLAIRE. She is dressed in modish black. Her
head is high, her face impassive like that of an
ancient idol. The procession crosses the stage and
goes off. The PEOPLE bow in silence as the coffin
passes. When they have boarded the train, the
STATION MASTER blows a long blast.)

STATION MASTER. Güllen-Rome Express. All aboard,
please!

(He holds up his paddle. [SOUND CUE # 36.] The
TRAIN starts, and moves off slowly, picking up
speed. The CROWD turns slowly, gazing after the
departing train in complete silence. The TRAIN
sounds fade.)

SLOW CURTAIN

END OF THE PLAY

SONGS FOR "THE VISIT"

ANCIENT FOLK SONG WITH THE AMENDED WORDS

Thank you, dear lady, for visiting our home town,
    Güllen Town,
Welcome, oh welcome, Claire Zachanassian, we
 sing out the paean of your renown, great renown—
Ding dong bell, hope you're well,
Bell dong ding, our hearts sing, home is the place
    we love best.
Ding dong bell, hope you're well,
Bell dong ding our hearts sing,
Welcome back home to the nest. Pom, Pom.

(This song is sung by the Mixed Choir in the 1st Railroad Station scene and is sung later in the 1st act when Claire Zachanassian is making her entrance for the banquet scene.)

THE HAPPY WANDERER

I love to go a-wandering upon the
    mountain high
And as I go I love to sing beneath God's
    clear blue sky
Falderi
Falderi
Faldera
Faldera
Falderi
Falderi
Faldera-ah-ah-ah-ah-ah-ah-ah-AH!

SONG TO BE SUNG BY THE TWO LITTLE GIRLS
UNDER THE BALCONY TO
CLAIRE ZACHANASSIAN.

Like a thought in the night we come
Like a phantom we wait
Like a bell tolling under the sea
Telling you it's too late . . .

But laugh now, you need no tears,
Clara is setting you free . . .

(Schill enters at this point. The girls scream and exit followed by the Teacher.)

(The children return and complete the song.)
Round the world she carried your song
And tore the oceans apart
But come now, loveliest flower
So will she tear out your heart.

SOUND PLOT

NOTE: *Master gain* must be full for all trains.

Cue No.	Description	Cue No.	Description
1	Express passing	21A	Chords
2	Express passing	22	Church Music
2A	Puffing train passing	23	New Bell
3	Express stopping	24	Fels Background
3A	Steam	25	Express Passing
4	Express starting	25A	Express Passing
5	Puffing train passing	25B	Express Passing
6	Church bell	26	Local arriving
7	Fels Background	27	Local departing
8	March		*End of Act Two*
9	Panther	28	Fels Background
	Then:	29	Chords
	Fels Background	30	Bells of Güllen
12	Cuckoo	31	Greek Tune
13	March	32	Fels Dramatic
14	Fanfare	33	Heimat Dramatic
	End of Act One	34	Radio Pips
15	Greek Tune	35	Express Stopping
16	Greek Tune	35A	Church Bells
17	Greek Tune	36	Train starting
18	Greek Tune		(As final curtain
19	Merry Widow		descends, fade Cues
20	Merry Widow		35A and 36)
21	Chords		

NOTE: The woodpecker effect in Act 2 was achieved with a wooden toy woodpecker, obtainable in most toy shops. The station bell (with hammer) is placed in the last bay Left and hung on the Left portal.

NOTE: *For details on rental of sound recording, cued as above to text of this book, write to:*

ROBERT WHITEHEAD
1501 Broadway
New York, N.Y. 10036

PRODUCTION NOTE

Regarding the Over-All Approach to Staging "The Visit"

by JOSEPH BROWNSTONE, *Stage Manager*

As will be noted in reading the stage directions of THE VISIT, as well as in reading the descriptions of the various settings, and in the scrutiny of the ground plans to be found in the back of this script, the over-all concept in staging THE VISIT requires a fluidity of movement by all the actors, as well as in the lighting and in the transitions from one scene to another. This is essential throughout each and every scene of the play. It is all-important. It is because of this concept that it is vital that each actor be specifically assigned various duties, involving the striking of scenery and properties and also in terms of bringing on and setting different units.

(As originally presented in New York City, as well as on the national tour of THE VISIT, there were only several places where the actors were not involved in the shifting of scenery (other than the lighting and the fly cues) and that was the scene strike at the conclusion of the Act 3 shop scene and the shift at the very end of the play for the curtain calls. The only other scene changes not involving actors were the onstage and offstage shifts of the Left and Right station units, and the various shifts of the balcony unit.)

It will therefore be of the utmost importance to consider all the technical aspects of the production most carefully and in great detail in working out the casting, the lighting, the sound, the scene shifts, the costume changes, etc. since the very nature and concept of THE VISIT necessitates a close and careful working relationship between all departments.

A NOTE REGARDING THE CASTING OF THE PRODUCTION

In the original production of THE VISIT as well as in the National Touring Company, many of the roles were doubled and tripled, allowing the size of the cast to be considerably reduced. The following is suggested as a possible and practical solution for limiting the size of the cast:

MAX—Can also be cast as a townsman in the tribunal scene.

Can also be cast as an athlete for the first half of the banquet scene.

Can also be cast as a townesman in the 2nd Railroad Station scene.

MIKE—Same as above.

FIRST BLINDMAN—Can also be cast as a townsman in the 2nd Railroad Scene.

Can also be cast as a radio reporter in the tribunal scene.

SECOND BLINDMAN—Can also be cast as a townsman in the 2nd Railroad Scene.

Can also be cast as a spot lamp operator in the tribunal scene.

THE SON—Can also be cast as a townsman in the 2nd Railroad Scene.

Can also be cast as a townsman in the Tribunal Scene.

THE THIRD MAN—Can also be cast as The Delivery Man.

THE SECOND WOMAN—Can also be cast as The Frau Burgomaster.

Can also be cast as a Reporter in the Tribunal Scene.

THE FIRST GRANDCHILD—Can also be cast as the Photographer in the Tribunal Scene.

THE STATION MASTER—Can appear as a member of the Tribunal.

THE CONDUCTOR—Can appear as a townsman in the Banquet Scene.

Can also be cast as a townsman in the 2nd Railroad Scene.

Can also be cast as a townsman in the Tribunal Scene.

THE REPORTER—Can appear as a townsman and member of the choir in the 1st Railroad Scene. Also, as a member of the band in the Banquet Scene. Also, as Townsman throughout the second act prowl scenes and as the camera operator during the Tribunal Scene and as a townsman in the final railroad scene.

THE TRUCKDRIVER—Can appear as a townsman in all scenes, except the 2nd Railroad scene.

THE ATHLETE—Can also be cast as a townsman throughout, including the tribunal scene, in which he can appear as a member of the tribunal and the one who actually strangles Anton Schill.

It is further recommended that when the size of your cast is limited and the assistant stage manager is serving as a member of the cast, that he be assigned the role of the Conductor. A break-down of his duties will appear elsewhere in this script.

PRODUCTION NOTES

Regarding Station Units, Restaurant Units, Balcony Unit, ond Other Units:

1. The Left and Right Station Units, consist of painted flats, and each is mounted on platform units with casters to enable the units to be moved on and off stage quickly and quietly. The off stage ends of each platform has a long paddle hinged to the platform which is used as a handle to help push the units on stage or to pull them off stage and prevents the audience from seeing the operators of these units.

2. The Left and Right Restaurant Units, consist of painted flats, and each is mounted on platform units with casters.

   NOTE: These units are moved onstage and offstage only one time during the play. They should be moved onstage simultaneously with the lowering of the center restaurant unit representing the doorway (Fly Cue No. 3). If there are no facilities for flying the center unit, it is suggested that the center unit be mounted on a platform unit with casters and that this unit should work simultaneously with the Left and Right units when being brought onstage. This would necessitate that the center unit be brought on from the 5th Bay Left. (This, because Claire Zachanassian enters through the center unit doorway, coming from the 5th Bay Right.)

3. The balcony unit is an easily assembled unit, also constructed on a platform with casters to enable easy operation. This has an additional escape stair unit which can be folded up when balcony unit is not in use.

   NOTE: This unit can remain in one position throughout the entire second act and only at the end of the second act, prior to the railroad station scene can it be moved up stage. When this occurs,

95

the backdrop, as shown on the ground plan, center panel drop is lowered. This should be done only when the second act railroad scene is about to take place. Therefore, Balcony Cues No. 1 through No. 5 can be eliminated and the balcony unit can remain in the downstage position until Balcony Cue No. 6. Fly Cue No. 9, discussed elsewhere, which affects the lowering of the center panel drop, should not be given until the balcony unit has been rolled upstage (Balcony Cue No. 6).

4. The counter unit is constructed on casters, as is the desk unit which is utilized in the police station scene.

5. The signal light which is pre-set on the D L corner of the large table for the tribunal scene, has a red and green light attached to the unit. As the stenographer, who enters from R No. 1 carrying the microphone and the cable reaches the center table in the tribunal scene, she hooks up the microphone cable to the signal light, the red light should light up when she moves away to her downstage R position, the radio man (1st Blindman) signals the Burgomaster to start speaking and the green light goes on and the red light goes off.

6. The two (2) downstage lampposts L and R work as one unit.

7. The two (2) upstage lampposts L and R work as one unit and move up and down simultaneously with the downstage lampposts. These lampposts are all practical. The upstage lampposts are different inasmuch as they have huge threefold replica of the buildings of the town, with practical lights shining through the windows of the representational houses.

ASSISTANT STAGE MANAGER CUES AND BUSINESS

(Performing as the Conductor)

ACT ONE

1. *On Cue:* From Stage Manager: Hit Station Bell with hammer until the Station Master salutes.

2. *On Cue:* "watching trains"*—Hit Station Bell with hammer until the Station Master salutes.

3. *On Cue:* "painting signs"*—Hit Station Bell with hammer until the Station Master salutes.

4. *On Cue:* "on that first impression"*—Hit Station Bell with hammer—2 Times.

5. *On Cue:* "if it only comes off"*—Hit Station Bell and continue until: "That's not her train" . . .

6. *On Cue:* "the ropes are fixed in time"*—Hit Station Bell until the 1st Man starts crossing upstage, saying: "Burgomaster"*

7. *On Cue:* (Mixed Choir Song) "Welcome, Oh, Wel—* Come . . ." continues hitting Station Bell until ". . . our heart's sing* . . ."

ACT TWO

1. *On Cue:* As Policeman starts to pour beer—Hand signal to Schill (who is behind Balcony Unit) to enter. Signal to him from 4th Bay L.

2. *On Cue:* As 2nd Man picks up Altar Cloth and *starts* to roll counter off give cue for the two gun shots. (This action can best be observed from 3rd Bay L.

3. Hold flashlight for Claire Zachanassian's exit from balcony, and as the actres clears the escape stair unit, strike the stair unit towards stage right, enabling the handlers of the balcony unit to strike that unit upstage.

4. *On Cue:* Doctor: " . . . Hold up letters, what an idea*." Hit Station Bell, continuing until townsmen are half-way into line-up, then enter from 1st Bay L and join in the line-up.

97

5. *On Cue:* As Schill reaches full standing position, hand signal to Truck Driver to Re-enter from Station House L. Stand in 3rd Bay L to signal him.

ACT THREE

1. *On Cue:* Teacher sits after "I have nothing more to say." Hand signal (from 1st Bay L) for Reporter to make his entrance.

2. *On Cue:* Schill sits on forest bench. Hand signal (from 1st Bay L) to Claire Zachanassian to enter from 5th Bay R.

3. On blackout after Burgomaster receives check from Bobby, help Anton Schill exit between D L lamppost and station truck to 4th Bay L.

> NOTE: The above-listed duties of the Assistant Stage Manager do not include the other pieces of business which are shown in the script itself, when performing as the Conductor, or as a Townsman and handling furniture, properties, etc.

PROPERTY PLOT

Stage Left:
Camera on tripod
Spot Lamp
Stepladder
2 Brooms
1 Can of Butter (on shelf, 1st Bay L)
Sedan Chair
Bucket w/water (used for the prop "pike")
Fishing rod
Fishing net
Fishing Creel w/trout
Mandolin Case
Guitar Case
9 Straightback chairs
Large table
14 pieces of luggage, matching
Panther cage w/cover
Coffin w/cover
Bass drum w/stick
Snare drum w/sticks
Trumpet
Sousaphone
Green flag on pole
Green banner w/initials C Z
Straw basket w/pitchfork
Small wicker basket
Swivel chair on casters
12 prop rifles
Camera w/flash gun
2 dusters
Water decanter and glass w/water

Burgomaster's mace
Red and green signal lights (practical) for tribunal table
Beer Mug
Mandolin
Guitar
2 tablecloths, 1 large, 1 small
1 wine bottle w/wine (practical)
Wooden tray w/:3 champagne glasses, 3 silver plates and wooden gavel
Wooden tray w/:9 glasses, 6 plates, assorted silver
Cornstraw broom
Small cardboard box of flags and flowers
Shop counter on casters w/:
   Cashbook and pencil
   2 milk cans, ladle (under counter)
   Aluminum tray w/ weight (scale) (under counter)
Wagonwheels
Set of shop shelves on casters w/:
   Bottom Shelf:
      2 large glass jars
      Assorted loaves of bread

99

Bread knife
Duster
Dustpan and brush
6 bottles (glued)
1 spare pencil
2 glasses
Second Shelf:
Box cigars (practical)
Numerous cigarette packs including green box
3 packets tobacco
Assorted dressing

Third Shelf:
Numerous bottles including:
2 cognac, 1 Steinhager
2 Schnapps
2 boxes dummy
2 practical chocolate bars
Assorted dressing
1 Lamplighter's pole
2 ratchets (noisemakers)
1 small table
1 .32 cal. blank pistol w/2 blanks

Stage Right:
Stepladder
Typewriter in wrapping paper
1 small table
Radio control box w/headphones on chair
Microphone attached to above with 20′ electric cord
2 lamplighter's poles
1 Champagne bottle (practical) in ice bucket
Towel
10 straightback chairs
1 Television set tied to a small hand truck
2 shopping bags
2 small milk pails
Numerous music sheets (for distribution to townspeople)
Duster
Streamers, blowers, noisemakers
Small gasoline can
Altar cloth
Bible, Liturgy and Psalter
1 Mop
1 crate eggs
1 camera (for Pedro)
2 wreaths
Tray w/tea set for two (practical)
Policeman's desk on casters w/:
Straight back chair on desk top

French telephone on small shelf under desk top
Beer bottle open (practical) on small shelf under desk
    top
Glass
Notebook and pencil
Wheelbarrow
Burlap
Wooden bucket
2 wine bottles (practical)
Wooden tray w/: 9 glasses, 6 plates, assorted silver, table-
    cloth
Banner with THANK YOU, FAREWELL
Fahrplan

PRESET ON STAGE
(ACT I)

Bench
2 wooden boxes
Luggage truck
4 cans paint w/brushes
1 Banner lettered: one side, WELCOME CLARA; other
    side, WELCOME MA
Station paddle hanging on Station Master's shack
2 banner poles, one on each truck, inboard
Small table
1 chair
2 beer mugs
1 broom leaning against left station unit

PRESET ON STAGE
(ACT II)

Strike all dishes and restaurant furniture
Counter on marks w/broom, dustpan and brush, cash-
    book and pencil, Duster flush 2 milk cans and ladle on
    floor behind counter
2 Straw bottom chairs (shop chairs only)
On Balcony:
    2 wrought iron chairs
    Small table w/cloth
Bench on shop marks (diagonal)

Stepladder in 1st Bay Left
Strike flags and flowers from station units
Set new Güllen sign on Left Station Unit; FAHRPLAN
  on Right Station Unit
Policeman's rifle set in 4th Bay L

PRESET ON STAGE
(ACT III)
Preset stage left, 4th Bay, counter and shelves
Preset stage Right, 1st Bay; bench
Sedan chair on marks (diagonal)
Wagonwheels (USC)
Small wicker basket
Wooden bucket
Large straw basket w/pitchfork
Wheelbarrow w/burlap
Set banner (THANK YOU, FAREWELL) on poles on L
  and R station units
Set Christmas garlands on station units in wings

* * * * * * * * * *

At the end of the shop scene, two (2) property men
strike the shelves and counter in the blackout.

After the final curtain, a property man strikes the
bench into the 1st Bay R, the other stagehands strike the
L and R station units into the wings, the lampposts are
flown for the curtain calls.

PLOT OF PROP MOVEMENT
By ACTORS

ACT I, *Scene 1*
Brooms used and struck by 2nd, 3rd and 4th man
Ladders used by 1st and 2nd man—struck by 2nd and 4th
    man
Boxes struck by 3rd man and 2nd child
Paint pots struck by painter
Banner struck by painter
Chair set by stationmaster—struck by 1st child

ACT I, *Scene 2*
Bench moved to 1st forest marks by 1st child
Luggage carried from Left to Right by:
    FRAU SCHILL

    PAINTER   Coffin
    2ND MAN

    2ND CHILD
    1ST CHILD (*Enters from* R.)
    OTTILIE
    3RD MAN
    KARL
    CONDUCTOR
    1ST MAN

    REPORTER   Panther Cage
    ATHLETE
Table moved down by Burgomaster and Teacher—Struck
    by Athlete and Third Man
Chairs moved down by Burgomaster and Teacher—struck
    by Conductor and Station Master

ACT I, *Scene 3*
Sedan Chair carried on and off by Mike and Max

ACT I, *Scene 4*
Chairs set by 1st Woman, 3rd Man and 1st Man

103

Small Table Left set by 2nd and 4th Man
Small Table Right set by 1st Man and Conductor
Center Table set by Station Master and Conductor
ACT II, *Scene 1*
1 shop chair is struck by Conductor

ACT II, *Scene 2* (Police Station)
Shop shelves struck by conductor and painter
Small Desk with phone, bottle beer, mug, notebook and
    chair rolled on and set by policeman
Conductor strikes phone into desk drawer
Reporter closes police register and removes it w/bottle
    and mug and pencil
3rd Man wheels TV across from R 4 to L 1

ACT II, *Scene 3*—(Burgomaster's Office)
Swivel chair—Rolled on by Burgomaster
Burgomaster's swivel chair is struck by 1st Man
Police Station desk is struck by 2nd Man
Shop chair is struck by 3rd Man

ACT II, *Scene 4*—(Church)
Bench is re-set by Reporter
Altar and altar cloth struck by 2nd Man

ACT III, *Scene 1*—(Great Barn)
Barrel is struck by Teacher
Basket is struck by Doctor
Wagon Wheels are struck by Athlete
Basket and Rake are struck by Station Master
Wheelbarrow is struck by 3rd Man

ACT III, *Scene 2*—(Schill's Shop)
Bench is set by 2nd Man
Counter is set by Conductor
Shelves are set by Karl and Painter

ACT III, *Scene 3*—(Woods)
Shelves are struck by Stagehand
Counter is struck by Stagehand

ACT III, *Scene 4*—(Tribunal-Golden Apostle-
Auditorium)
Chairs are set and struck by actors

Center Table w/water pitcher and glass and mace set by Truckdriver and Athlete

Newsreel Camera set and struck by Cameraman (Reporter)

Floodlight set and struck by (2nd Blind Man)

Radio set and struck by Radioman (1st Blind Man)

Microphone and cable set and struck by Stenographer (2nd woman)

FLY PLOT

ACT ONE

(*Pre-set Lamppost units*)
Fly Cue No. 1
    The upstage lampposts are flown out
    The Golden Apostle sign is flown in
Fly Cue No. 2
    The downstage lampposts are flown out
    The Golden Apostle sign is flown out
Fly Cue No. 3
    The center unit representing the doorway of the restaurant is flown in
    (*After the 1st act curtain, the center unit is flown out*)

ACT TWO

(*Pre-set Shop sign*) (*The center panel drop is flown out*)
Fly Cue No. 4
    The shop sign is flown out
Fly Cue No. 5
    The Police sign is flown in
Fly Cue No. 6
    The Police sign is flown out
Fly Cue No. 7
    The Rathaus sign is flown in
Fly Cue No. 8
    The Rathaus sign is flown out
Fly Cue No. 9
    The upstage and downstage lampposts are flown in and as soon as the balcony unit has been moved upstage, the center panel drop is flown in.
    (After the 2nd act curtain, the lampposts are flown out)

ACT THREE

(*Pre-set the barn ladder*)
Fly Cue No. 10

The barn ladder is flown out
The shop sign is flown in
Fly Cue No. 11
The shop sign is flown out
Fly Cue No. 12
The town hall lamps (8) are flown in
The town hall banner is flown in
Fly Cue No. 13
The town hall lamps are flown out
The town hall banner is flown out
The upstage and downstage lampposts are flown in
(*After the final curtain, the lampposts are flown
out quickly for the curtain calls*)

NOTE: For purposes of simplifying the production, it is suggested that the various signs denoting the different locales be limited. The barn ladder can also be eliminated. The center panel drop is essential for the second act balcony scenes and must be used after the balcony unit has been brought upstage beyond the backdrop. Depending upon the facilities in your individual theatre, a means of employing the lamppost units, as well as the town hall lamps and the town hall banner, would have to be worked out accordingly, or, perhaps eliminated.

*Regarding Fly Cue No. 3, if this were to present
a problem, it is suggested that this be utilized in
conjunction with the bringing on of the Left and
Right Restaurant units.*

TRUCK AND BALCONY CUES

ACT ONE

(*Pre-set* L *and* R *station units on stage*)
Truck Cue No. 1
  Station units move offstage into wings simultaneously

ACT TWO

Balcony Cue No. 1
  Balcony unit rolled downstage approximately 4 feet
Balcony Cue No. 2
  Balcony unit rolled upstage to marks
Balcony Cue No. 3
  Balcony unit rolled downstage approximately 4 feet
Balcony Cue No. 4
  Balcony unit rolled upstage to marks
Balcony Cue No. 5
  Balcony unit rolled downstage approximately 4 feet
Balcony Cue No. 6
  Balcony unit rolled upstage to marks
Truck Cue No. 2
  Station units moved onstage simultaneously
    (*At end of Act 2, station units are moved into wings.*
    Christmas tree lights garlands are placed on both
    station units for the Act 3 railroad station scene)

ACT THREE

Truck Cue No. 3
  Station units moved onstage simultaneously
    (*At end of railroad station scene, strike both*
    station units into wings for curtain calls)

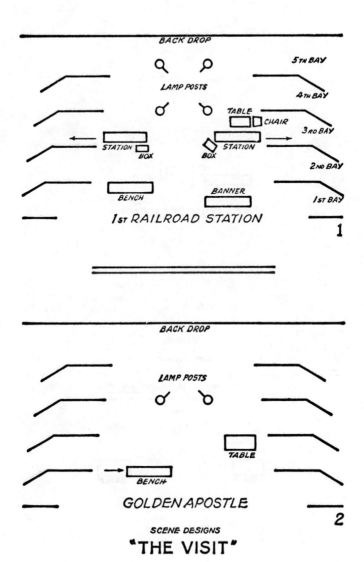

SCENE DESIGNS
"THE VISIT"

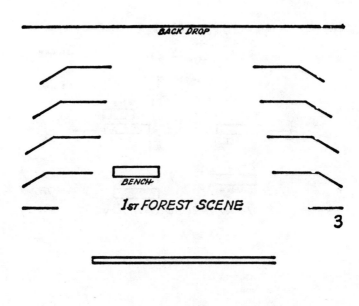

1st FOREST SCENE

3

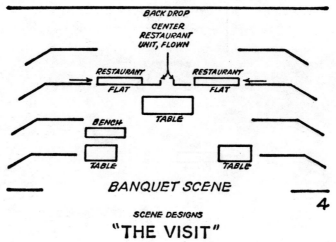

BANQUET SCENE

4

SCENE DESIGNS

"THE VISIT"

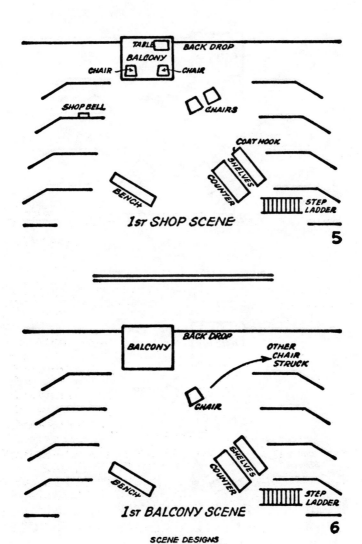

1st SHOP SCENE

5

1st BALCONY SCENE

6

SCENE DESIGNS
"THE VISIT"

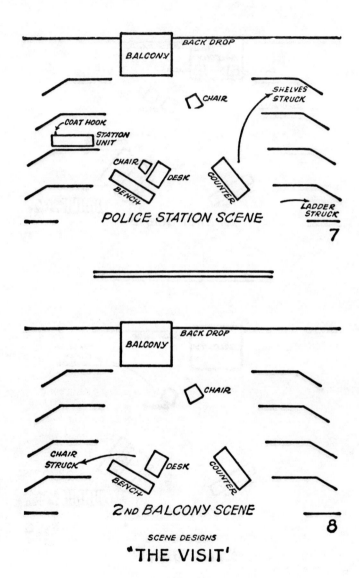

BALCONY BACK DROP

CHAIR

SHELVES STRUCK

COAT HOOK STATION UNIT

CHAIR DESK

BENCH

COUNTER

LADDER STRUCK

POLICE STATION SCENE

7

BALCONY BACK DROP

CHAIR

CHAIR STRUCK

DESK

BENCH

COUNTER

2ND BALCONY SCENE

8

SCENE DESIGNS
'THE VISIT'

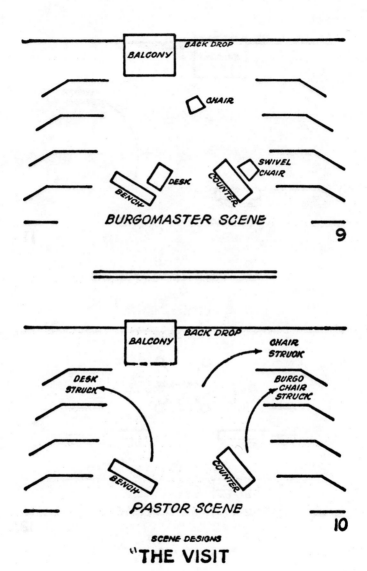

BACK DROP

BALCONY

CHAIR

SWIVEL
CHAIR

BENCH   DESK   COUNTER

BURGOMASTER SCENE

9

BACK DROP

BALCONY

CHAIR
STRUCK

DESK
STRUCK

BURGO
CHAIR
STRUCK

BENCH   COUNTER

PASTOR SCENE

10

SCENE DESIGNS
"**THE VISIT**

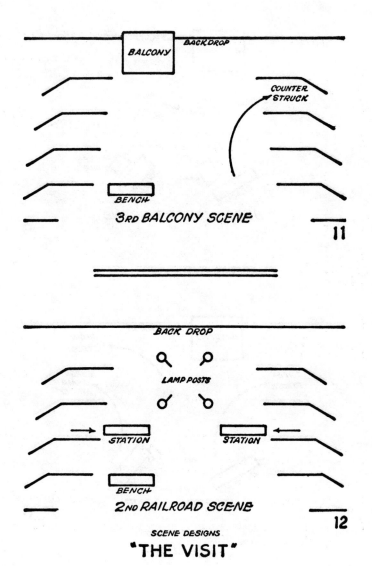

SCENE DESIGNS
"THE VISIT"

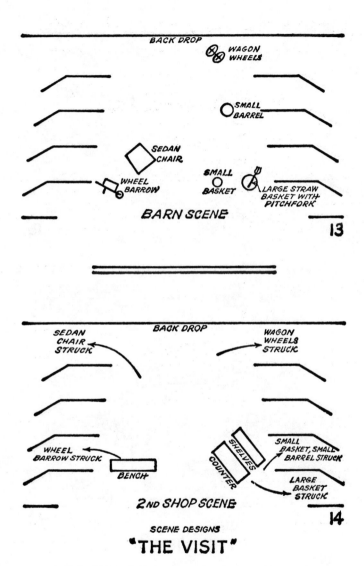

BACK DROP

WAGON
WHEELS

SMALL
BARREL

SEDAN
CHAIR

WHEEL
BARROW

SMALL
BASKET

LARGE STRAW
BASKET WITH
PITCHFORK

BARN SCENE

13

BACK DROP

SEDAN
CHAIR
STRUCK

WAGON
WHEELS
STRUCK

WHEEL
BARROW STRUCK

BENCH

SHELVES

COUNTER

SMALL
BASKET, SMALL
BARREL STRUCK

LARGE
BASKET
STRUCK

2ND SHOP SCENE

14

SCENE DESIGNS
"THE VISIT"

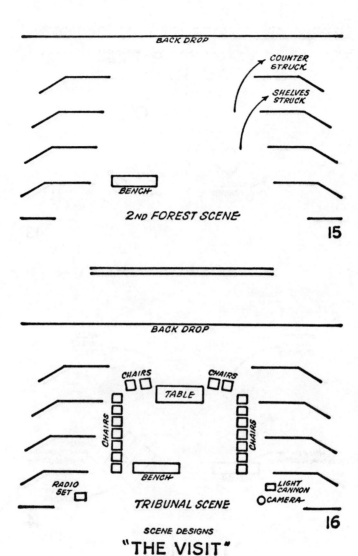

BACK DROP

COUNTER
STRUCK

SHELVES
STRUCK

BENCH

2ND FOREST SCENE

15

BACK DROP

CHAIRS   CHAIRS

TABLE

CHAIRS   CHAIRS

BENCH

RADIO
SET

LIGHT
CANNON

CAMERA

TRIBUNAL SCENE

16

SCENE DESIGNS

"THE VISIT"

Other Publications for Your Interest

TALKING WITH . . .

(LITTLE THEATRE)

By JANE MARTIN

11 women—Bare stage

Here, at last, is the collection of eleven extraordinary monologues for eleven actresses which had them on their feet cheering at the famed Actors Theatre of Louisville—audiences, critics and, yes, even jaded theatre professionals. The mysteriously pseudonymous Jane Martin is truly a ''find'', a new writer with a wonderfully idiosyncratic style, whose characters alternately amuse, move and frighten us always, however, speaking to use from the depths of their souls. The characters include a baton twirler who has found God through twirling; a fundamentalist snake handler, an ex-rodeo rider crowded out of the life she has cherished by men in 3-piece suits who want her to dress up ''like Minnie damn Mouse in a tutu''; an actress willing to go to any length to get a job; and an old woman who claims she once saw a man with ''cerebral walrus'' walk into a McDonald's and be healed by a Big Mac. ''Eleven female monologues, of which half a dozen verge on brilliance.''—London Guardian. ''Whoever (Jane Martin) is, she's a writer with an original imagination.''—Village Voice. ''With Jane Martin, the monologue has taken on a new poetic form, intensive in its method and revelatory in its impact.''—Philadelphia Inquirer. ''A dramatist with an original voice . . . (these are) tales about enthusiasms that become obsessions, eccentric confessionals that levitate with religious symbolism and gladsome humor.''—N.Y. Times. *Talking With . . .* is the 1982 winner of the American Theatre Critics Association Award for Best Regional Play.　　　　　　　　　　　　　　(#22009)

HAROLD AND MAUDE

(ADVANCED GROUPS—COMEDY)

By COLIN HIGGINS

9 men, 8 women—Various settings

Yes: *the Harold and Maude!* This is a stage adaptation of the wonderful movie about the suicidal 19-year-old boy who finally learns how to truly *live* when he meets up with that delightfully whacky octogenarian, Maude. Harold is the proverbial Poor Little Rich Kid. His alienation has caused him to attempt suicide several times, though these attempts are more cries for attention than actual attempts. His peculiar attachment to Maude, whom he meets at a funeral (a mutual passion), is what saves him—and what captivates us. This new stage version, a hit in France directed by the internationally-renowned Jean-Louis Barrault, will certainly delight both afficionados of the film and new-comers to the story. ''Offbeat upbeat comedy.''—Christian Science Monitor.　　　　　　　　(#10032)

ARCHANGELS DON'T PLAY PINBALL

(LITTLE THEATRE—FARCE WITH MUSIC)

BY DARIO FO

Translated by Ron Jenkins

7 men, 3 women—Various ints. and exts.

First performed in September 1986 at the Bristol Old Vic, this fast-moving play is one of Fo's most accomplished farces and the first to combine political-satirical content with a Brechtian form—evident in the play's songs but also in its reliance on paradoxical situations to make its points. Set in the industrial outskirts of Milan, it follows the peripeteias of a group of louts and their butt, Lofty, a simple man caught in the maze of government bureaucracy trying to extricate himself from the desperate demi-mode of pranks and petty crimes. The piece is unusual in that the cast often (seven men and three women) all, with the exception of the hero and his girlfriend, play numerous parts. This doubling is used as a source of farcical complication for the hero keeps recognizing the players in their new guises. "The piece is genial...This is a very friendly Fo." The Guardian. "...exuberant in its good-natured teasing of bureaucracy and authority...zany energy." Daily Telegraph.

ELIZABETH: ALMOST BY CHANCE A WOMAN

(ADVANCED GROUPS)

BY DARIO FO

Translated by Ron Jenkins with assistance from Arturo Curso

6 men, 2 women—Unit Set

This hilarious farce focuses on Elizabeth I of England. It's a devastating satire on politics in the Age of Reagan. Elizabeth is this aging, forgetful monarch, see, who is obsessed with appearances. She is also suspicious of artists such as Shakespeare, who has written a play about some Danish prince which Elizabeth in convinced is really about *her*. The play is performed for her in a hilarious parody of *Hamlet*, strained through the garbled pidgin-English of Mama Zaza, a drag queen who has earlier told us that the play we are about to see has absolutely nothing to do with Reagan. "Fo nails pretension and political chicanery with ridicule, laughter, sarcasm, irony and the grotesque...This being Fo, the play is rich with raunch and scatology—may offend the unwary. But for Fo converts, it's a must, just as it's an ideal introduction to one of the world's funniest theatre satirists."—Variety.

Other Publications for Your Interest

CINDERELLA WALTZ
(ALL GROUPS—COMEDY)
By DON NIGRO

4 men, 5 women—1 set

Rosey Snow is trapped in a fairy tale world that is by turns funny and a little frightening, with her stepsisters Goneril and Regan, her demented stepmother, her lecherous father, a bewildered Prince, a fairy godmother who sings salty old sailor songs, a troll and a possibly homicidal village idiot. A play which investigates the archetypal origins of the world's most popular fairy tale and the tension between the more familiar and charming Perrault version and the darker, more ancient and disturbing tale recorded by the brothers Grimm. Grotesque farce and romantic fantasy blend in a fairy tale for adults.

(#5208)

ROBIN HOOD
(LITTLE THEATRE—COMEDY)
By DON NIGRO

14 men, 8 women—(more if desired.) Unit set.

In a land where the rich get richer, the poor are starving, and Prince John wants to cut down Sherwood Forest to put up an arms manufactory, a slaughterhouse and a tennis court for the well to do, this bawdy epic unites elements of wild farce and ancient popular mythologies with an environmentalist assault on the arrogance of wealth and power in the face of poverty and hunger. Amid feeble and insane jesters, a demonic snake oil salesman, a corrupt and lascivious court, a singer of eerie ballads, a gluttonous lusty friar and a world of vivid and grotesque characters out of a Brueghel painting, Maid Marian loses her clothes and her illusions among the poor and Robin tries to avoid murder and elude the Dark Monk of the Wood who is Death and also perhaps something more.

(#20075)

Other Publications for Your Interest

OTHER PEOPLE'S MONEY
(LITTLE THEATRE—DRAMA)
By JERRY STERNER

3 men, 2 women—One Set

Wall Street takeover artist Lawrence Garfinkle's intrepid computer is going "tilt" over the undervalued stock of New England Wire & Cable. He goes after the vulnerable company, buying up its stock to try and take over the company at the annual meeting. If the stockholders back Garfinkle, they will make a bundle—but what of the 1200 employees? What of the local community? Too bad, says Garfinkle, who would then liquidate the company—take the money and run. Set against the charmingly rapacious financier are Jorgenson, who has run the company since the Year One and his chief operations officer, Coles, who understands, unlike the genial Jorgenson, what a threat Garfinkle poses to the firm. They bring in Kate, a bright young woman lawyer, who specializes in fending off takeovers—and who is the daughter of Jorgenson's administrative assistant, Bea. Kate must not only contend with Garfinkle—she must also move Jorgenson into taking decisive action. Should they use "greenmail"? Try to find a "White Knight"? Employ a "shark repellent"? This compelling drama about Main Street vs. Wall Street is as topical and fresh as today's headlines, giving its audience an inside look at what's *really going on* in this country and asking trenchant questions, not the least of which is whether a corporate raider is really the creature from the Black Lagoon of capitalism or the Ultimate Realist come to save business from itself.

(#17064)

THE DOWNSIDE
(LITTLE THEATRE—COMEDY)
By RICHARD DRESSER

6 men, 2 women—Combination Interior

These days, American business is a prime target for satire, and no recent play has cut as deep, with more hilarious results, than this superb new comedy from the Long Wharf Theatre, Mark & Maxwell, a New Jersey pharmaceuticals firm, has acquired U.S. rights to market an anti-stress drug manufactured in Europe, pending F.D.A. approval; but the marketing executives have got to come up with a snazzy ad campaign by January—and here we are in December! The irony is that nowhere is this drug more needed than right there at Mark & Maxwell, a textbook example of corporate ineptitude, where it seems all you have to do to get ahead is look good in a suit. The marketing strategy meetings get more and more pointless and frenetic as the deadline approaches. These meetings are "chaired" by Dave, the boss, who is never actually there—he is a voice coming out of a box, as Dave phones in while jetting to one meeting or another, eventually directing the ad campaign on his mobile phone while his plane is being hijacked! Doesn't matter to Dave, though—what matters is the possible "downside" of this new drug: hallucinations. "Ridiculous", says the senior marketing executive Alan: who then proceeds to tell how Richard Nixon comes to his house in the middle of the night to visit…"Richard Dresser's deft satirical sword pinks the corporate image repeatedly, leaving the audience amused but thoughtful."—Meriden Record. "Funny and ruthlessly cynical."—Phila. Inquirer. "A new comedy that is sheer delight."—Westport News. "The Long Wharf audience laughed a lot, particularly those with office training. But they were also given something to ponder about the way we get things done in America these days, or rather pretend to get things done. No wonder the Japanese are winning."—L.A. Times.

(#6718)